Mind Over Matter

Liz MacLaren

BROCKHAMPTON PRESS
LONDON

This edition published 1996 by Brockhampton Press, a member of
the Hodder Headline PLC Group

ISBN 1 86019 385 4

Printed and bound in India

Contents

Contents

Introduction

It is difficult to be precise about what we mean by the word 'mind'. As with most words that we use frequently in the course of our everyday lives we use it without thinking. The word simply comes automatically to our lips in certain contexts and these contexts are not always the same.

We use it in connection with the reasoning processes and our powers of understanding. Thus we speak of 'mulling things over in our minds', of an adult being brain-damaged and having 'the mind of a child', and of people looking for jobs in which they can 'use their minds'.

In an extension of this meaning, we also use 'mind' to describe thoughts or attention. If school pupils are staring vacantly out of the window they might be told to 'keep their minds on their work'; it might be said of a girl that 'her mind was completely taken up with her wedding preparations'.

Our ability to remember is also sometimes ascribed to the mind. We speak of being unable to 'call something to mind' or say that 'someone puts us in mind of someone else'. Often we find that something 'has slipped our minds'.

Mind is often used more to indicate the powers of the imagination than the powers of reasoning and understanding. We might speak of seeing something 'in our mind's eye', an ability that is of great use to creative people, or tell a friend that her feeling that her boss disliked her was 'all in the mind'.

Decisions, intention and determination are also related linguistically to the mind. We can 'make up our minds to go', we frequently 'have it in mind' to do things and we can 'have a mind to take a holiday'.

Clearly the word 'mind' is a useful and versatile word. Where would we be without it? More importantly, where would we be without the faculties to which the word refers? The answer does not bear thinking about—in a zombie-like state at best.

As has been mentioned above, we use the word 'mind' to indicate intellectual powers, the power to think and reason. Thus we speak of someone 'having a good mind'. This, of course, refers not to the moral nature of someone's mind but to his or her exceptional powers of reasoning or intellectual ability. An alternative possibility is that the person in question has a 'fine mind'.

'Mind' in this context can become personified. The mind becomes the whole person when we speak of someone being 'one of the finest minds of the century' or use a number of similar phrases. This idea is used humorously in the well-known saying 'Great minds think alike', to which the reply is usually 'Fools seldom differ'.

In this context 'mind' is virtually synonymous with the word 'brain'. The words, however, are by no means interchangeable in all contexts. Far from it. We do not speak of having receiving 'mind damage' in an accident or of being operated on by a famous 'mind surgeon'.

When it comes to defining terms we are on much surer ground with the brain. The word can be used figuratively in the context mentioned above, in the same way that 'mind' can, in that we can speak of someone being 'one of the great brains of his or her generation' and of someone being 'the brains behind a scheme or organization'. However, unlike the mind, the brain is something tangible.

The brain has a fixed location—in our heads. Surgeons can operate on it, radiologists can X-ray it, and pathologists can remove it after death. There is no doubt about it. We know it is there.

The mind and brain, of course, have very close associations, indeed inseparable associations. Without the physical brain there would be no mind, and in a way the mind can be seen as the abstract form of the brain, both being central to the thinking process.

As scientific attention concentrates more and more on the physical properties and workings of the brain, more and more is being learnt about the function of the brain and the way in which it affects the rest of the body. Physiological reasons are coming to light for things that always seemed to be the case but could never be proved. For example, it is now thought that the body's ability to control its own pain levels in certain situations is a result of chemicals released by the brain.

Such demonstrations of the brain's ability is casting new light on old assumptions and in several cases is vindicating these. Thus it is now regarded as being likely that substances released by the brain can bring about certain states that were hitherto thought by some to be the product of the imagination. More information is given on this in Chapter 7, The Mind's Role in Illness and Health.

In other words, some recent scientific findings seem to have rationalized what has long been thought to be the case. It has long been felt that the mind could play a significant part in the state of health of the physical body. Science seems to be intent on proving this, except that it now appears, in some cases at least, that it is the physical brain rather than the abstract mind that is having this effect.

So far the meaning of the word 'mind' has been considered? But what about the word 'matter'? In many ways it appears to be more difficult.

Like 'mind', 'matter' has several meanings but only one is really relevant in the present context. This is rather a vague meaning and is often expressed as contrasting with 'mind'. The *Oxford Advanced Learner's Dictionary* defines matter in the present context as 'physical substance in general, contrasted with the mind or spirit'.

In Chapter 7, The Mind's Role in Illness and Health, this book discusses the power of the mind over matter when the matter involved is the human body. It has been shown that in some cases long-held assumptions might have to be rewritten to give the credit not to the abstract mind but to the physical brain and that scientific research will very probably continue in this process of demonstrating the multi-functions and the power of the brain.

Scientists on the whole are happier with concrete things. They like to be able to prove things and to have things crystal clear. That is why most of them would rather deal with the brain than with the mind.

However, there are several situations in which the mind seems to have a power over some form of matter, which science cannot yet explain. Many scientists, and indeed many non-scientists, feel extremely uncomfortable about this and treat such seeming instances of the mind's power over matter with great scepticism, if not ridicule.

One of these instances is psychokinesis, the seeming power of the human mind to influence the physical world. This claimed power of the mind over physical objects is supposedly at work in metal-bending. In metal-bending the person demonstrating his or her skill tries to make a piece of metal, such as a fork, spoon or metal bar, bend either without touching it at all or without exerting any physical force on it—sometimes he or she strokes it.

Metal-bending received a great deal of media attention in the 1970s and 1980s when Uri Geller was demonstrating his feats. These seemed to include mending broken watches without touching them as well as bending forks. When he demonstrated his art on television, some of the viewers even claimed that the forks in their kitchens began to bend of their own accord, and that grandfather clocks that had stopped years ago began chiming.

Uri Geller had many admirers but he had many detractors. Some have argued that because of all the media hype his powers were never properly tested or researched. More information on this and on metal-bending generally is given in Chapter 6, Psychokinesis.

Many tried to put Geller's seeming power over metal down to sleight of hand, although this in itself seems unlikely to account for all his feats. However, sceptics had more difficulty with the work of John Hasted, himself a scientist, who with the help of several subjects carried out experiments that seemed to demonstrate the power of the mind to affect metal in fairly spectacular ways. More information on this is given in Chapter 6, but one of the experiments involved getting his subject to put a collection of paper clips into a tangled cluster—when they were enclosed in a glass ball.

Demonstrations have also been given to try to prove that the human mind can move objects. One person who is said to have shown particular skill at this was a Russian woman called Nelya, or Nina, Kulagina. If she concentrated on certain reasonably small objects she is said to have been able to make them slide or roll. Indeed, it was said that she did not even have to concentrate. Her claimed gift is said to have been discovered when she was engaged on another extraordinary task, 'reading' a newspaper with her fingers. Small objects in the vicinity of this activity were supposedly seen to move slightly away. Again, more details about Kulagina are given in Chapter 6.

Another situation also supposedly involving moving objects is now thought to be the result of some activity in the human mind. Poltergeists, once thought to be demons and then thought to be the spirits of the dead, are now claimed by many parapsychologists to be the result of psychokinetic activity on the part of the mind of one of the people who live in the house affected. In houses supposedly subjected to poltergeist activity, rapping is heard behind the walls, objects fly across the room, other objects move to other rooms and stones are thrown at the outside walls. More information on poltergeist activity and its supposed causes is given in Chapter 1, Poltergeists.

These, then, are some of the ways in which the human mind is claimed to be able to gain victory over some form of matter. However, it is claimed that the human mind has other strange powers as well. Several people claim that the mind can leave the body and return to it again. This supposedly occurs during what is known as 'out-of-body experiences', when people claim to have been aware of floating up to the ceiling and of then looking down on their bodies below. More information is given in Chapter 5, Out-of-Body Experiences, which also deals with what are known as 'near-death experiences'.

The mind is claimed not only to be able to gain supremacy over metal and objects but to be able to defy our perceptions of time and space. Certain people are claimed to have some form of sense, other than the usual five senses, which enables them to perceive things that the rest of us cannot. This power is called extrasensory perception, the term being often abbreviated to ESP.

There are various forms of supposed ESP, and they can be categorized in various ways. In this book they have been categorized into telepathy, precognition and clairvoyance, and there are chapters on each of these headings.

In telepathy there is supposedly thought transference between two people who might be many miles apart. An example might be if someone suddenly felt in the middle of the night that a member of the family was in trouble and rushed round to the relevant house to discover that fire had broken out. Not all the claimed cases are as dramatic as that, but it acts as an illustration.

In instances of precognition, someone claims to have a vision, dream or premonition that something is going to happen in the future, which does actually happen. These are frequently related to disaster. For example, the sinking of the *Titanic* has many instances of supposed precognition attached to it. More information is given on this and the Aberfan disaster in Chapter 3, Precognition.

'Clairvoyance' is sometimes used rather loosely to refer to psychic power generally, and it is also sometimes used to mean much the same as precognition. In this book it is treated as a branch of ESP, being a claimed ability to detect or acquire information by some means other than through the five senses.

Because of this claimed ability, people often consult clairvoyants to help them locate missing persons. More macabrely, they are sometime called in to help find the bodies of people who are almost certainly dead. Clairvoyants are also sometimes asked to help in cases of crime detection, especially murder. They are often called in by relatives but sometimes by the police. For example, the Boston police called in a Dutch clairvoyant called Gerard Croiset to help them track down the murderer who became known as the Boston Strangler. More details are given in Chapter 4 Clairvoyance.

There are many accounts of feats claimed to be undertaken through the agency of the human mind that are quite amazing. There is no possible rational explanation for some of these as far as one can see, and in several cases there seems to be no possibility of fraud or hoax since they have been testified to by independent witnesses.

We are generally short of information in these paranormal fields, some more than others. It is felt by some parapsychologists that there are considerably more examples of precognition among ordinary people than is ever reported, partly because they are nervous of being labelled insane but perhaps because they are not sure to whom to report it. To obviate this latter possibility, there is the British Premonitions Bureau where people can register any serious premonitions or any dreams or visions that seem to predict the future.

It is tempting to treat all the supposedly paranormal fields with scepticism. We always prefer to dismiss that which we do not or cannot understand, but just because we do not understand something does not mean that it does not exist.

More information is needed and more research is required to be done on psychokinesis and ESP, but such research can be very expensive in times when there are so many calls on the money supply and compared with other things the paranormal is low-priority. For example, it can take considerable time and considerable expense, both in terms of personnel and equipment, to investigate a claim that a house is being subjected to poltergeist activity. Apart from anything else, there are a considerable number of frauds perpetrated in that field, often by children wishing to draw attention to themselves.

Researching poltergeists can be a slow process because apparently the activity often seems to die down when an investigator arrives. Cynics will doubtless say that this points to the fact that there is no such thing as poltergeist activity, but some investigators have reported that if they stay around long enough the activity resumes.

People involved in researching some aspect of the paranormal often comment on the fact that it is difficult to get ESP or psychokinesis to operate under test or laboratory conditions, that paranormal phenomena cannot be switched on and off like a tap. Clearly this would increase the amount of time and money involved in paranormal experiments and decrease our chances of getting much in the way of more information in the near future.

Research involving the mind and the human body, in which considerable progress has been made, has an inbuilt advantage. This research is related to health and so obviously takes a higher priority.

For the moment we must remain fairly ignorant about possible paranormal activity. There are certainly some accounts of supposed paranormal happenings for which there seems to be no normal, rational explanation, but you must make up your own minds. For my own part, I am a 'don't know' with occasional leanings towards a vague belief that there must be something in it.

Chapter 1

Poltergeists

The word 'poltergeist' is German for 'noisy spirit'. This is now something of a misnomer because, although not much is really known about what causes poltergeist activity, it is thought to be the result of some kind of paranormal psychokinetic activity relating to a human being rather than having anything to do with spirits.

Parapsychologists now frequently refer to poltergeist activity as Recurrent Spontaneous PK, PK being a common abbreviation of psychokinesis. Recurrent Spontaneous PK is often abbreviated to RSPK and is so called because of the recurrent aspect that characterizes poltergeist activity.

There has been much interest in poltergeists in the twentieth century, particularly in the later part of it, but poltergeists are far from being a recent phenomenon. They go back a very long way indeed.

Jacob Grimm in *Deutsche Mythologie* refers to an old German case of poltergeist activity that occurred in the year AD 355. The account by Grimm refers to a house having stones thrown at it and banging on its walls.

Perrault

The scientist Robert Boyle, who formulated Boyle's

Law in chemistry and who was one of the founders of the Royal Society in Britain, became interested in poltergeists in 1642 when he met a Huguenot minister called Francis Perrault whose household had been the victim of poltergeist activity. Perrault had written an account of the incidents relating to the poltergeist shortly after the strange activity had occurred and when the whole thing was still very fresh in his mind. Boyle was so impressed by the account that he arranged for it to be translated into English and published.

The first sign of unusual activity seemed to be directed at Perrault's maid and wife, and Perrault himself was inclined to view their accounts with scepticism. Soon, however, he himself witnessed the activity and reported hearing knocking and things being thrown. Eventually stones were being thrown at the house by day and night, and it was extremely difficult for anyone in the Perrault household to get any rest.

The poltergeist's actions affected the lives of the members of the Perrault household but the maid was the main focus of its activity. It would, for example, unmake beds that she had already made

In many ways the Perrault's poltergeist exhibited typical behaviour, and some of the activity usually associated with poltergeist activity is listed below, but there was one unusual feature associated with it. This was the fact that a human voice produced understandable words. Usually if there is vocal activity it takes the from of grunts or a few croaked, virtually incomprehensible words but the Perrault poltergeist seems to have been exceptionally talkative for a poltergeist.

Although poltergeist activity covers many hundreds of years and many countries there are remarkable similarities in the kind of activity that occurs when there is thought to be a poltergeist presence. These do not all always occur but they are very typical of the poltergeist experience.

Repetitiveness

As is suggested by the term that many modern parapsychologists use to describe claimed poltergeist activity—Recurrent Spontaneous PK—there is usually a marked repetitiveness associated with it. The activity often seems to start with a seemingly isolated incident or two but then it steps up, often with a vengeance. Poltergeist activity is usually fairly intensive for a varying, but usually relatively short, period of time, tending to last a few weeks or months.

In both these respects the house subjected to poltergeist activity is different from that subjected to haunting. Claimed apparitions give supposed evidence of their 'presence' far less frequently in a house than a poltergeist does but it does so over a much longer period of time. Some supposed ghosts have been reported appearing over several hundreds of years in some houses, although they might appear only once every few years.

Association with one person

When there is claimed to be poltergeist activity in a

house it usually seems to choose to focus on one person in particular. The poltergeist may seem to direct its activity towards all or several of the members of a household but, although it sometimes takes time for this to become obvious, there is often one person in particular who is the butt of the worst of its activity. As was the case in the Perrault case, where the main focus of poltergeist activity was the maid, the person at whom the poltergeist seems to direct the main thrust of its efforts is often a young woman or girl.

At least this used to be the case. Modern parapsychologists, however, think this may have shown signs of change in recent times. William Roll, once Director of the Psychical Research Foundation of North Carolina, estimated that up to this century about 80 per cent of poltergeist activity was focused on females but in this century the attention has been more evenly spread between the sexes.

Unlike claimed hauntings, which are place-related in that if a family moves away from a haunted house the haunting presence does not follow the family to their next house but stays where it is, in the poltergeist appears to be person-related. If it is the midst of a bout of activity and the person who is the main focus moves away it seems that the poltergeist moves with that person.

Julio

A very well-known case, well-known partly because it was carefully documented, demonstrated this tendency for poltergeist activity to follow one person if he or she leaves the original centre of its activity. Julio was a nineteen-year-old Cuban refugee who worked in a Miami warehouse.

I mention it here because, after some investigation was carried out at Julio's workplace and he was found to be the focus of poltergeist activity, Julio was asked to go the research centre at Durham, North Carolina, where the investigators worked so that further research could be carried out, specifically on the kind of personality with which poltergeist activity is often involved.

In Miami, when Julio was there, there had been much evidence of ornaments and glass objects getting broken. When he went to the research centre at Durham the poltergeist activity seemed to have followed him, and a large decorative vase standing on a table in a room near the doorway in which he was standing fell to the ground.

The Julio case is mentioned here because it demonstrates that poltergeist activity, especially when it is at its most aggressive, tends to follow the focus of its activity if he or she moves away in the course of its activity. It relates to a person rather than a place.

However, the case itself is interesting and one of the most famous for various reasons. It is thus worth recounting the whole story—or at least a truncated version of it.

In 1967 the owner of a Miami warehouse, Alvin Laubheim, called in the police because of the number of breakages that were occurring in his warehouse without explanation—there were many ornaments and souvenirs and much glassware in the building. He had originally thought that these breakages were due to carelessness among his shipping clerks but the sheer scale of the damage made him suspect that a ghost was at work.

Quite what he thought the Miami police could do about a ghost is not known. However, he called them in and they came, probably very reluctantly.

William Roll, then Director of Research at the Psychical Research Foundation of North Carolina, and someone with a great deal of experience of poltergeist research, happened to hear of this and decided to investigate. At first the poltergeist seemed shy of making his or her presence known in the presence of an investigator, a habit demonstrated by other poltergeists in similar circumstances.

However, much activity did eventually take place in Roll's presence, and often when he was keeping Julio under observation so that there was no possibility of a fraud involving Julio. Something strange was certainly going on but Julio certainly did not seem to be breaking things deliberately.

Roll arranged a series of objects on shelves throughout the warehouse, calling them target objects because he had positioned them in such a way that he would know if they had moved. One of these was an ashtray in the form of an alligator, and this was placed on a shelf in a part of the warehouse that had previously been the scene of much poltergeist activity. Julio placed a cowbell in front of it, the cowbell having been moved by seeming poltergeist activity several times before and so presumably a source of attraction to it.

It is reported by Roll that he was observing Julio in conversation with someone in the stockroom when an argument broke out and the alligator ashtray was heard to crash to the ground behind him. Roll continued to monitor other object movement or falls and found that the poltergeist was only active in Julio's presence.

Roll was so intrigued that he asked Julio to accompany him to his research centre in Durham, North Carolina. We have seen above how the poltergeist activity followed Julio there.

The investigators were particularly interested in Julio himself because they wanted to know if there was anything in his personality that might predispose him to poltergeist activity. He in no obvious way seemed disturbed and had functioned perfectly normally in his job, apart from the fact that he was deduced to be the centre of the poltergeist activity.

However, when he was subjected to psychological and personality tests he was found by two psychologists to be outwardly a passive, unemotional person who had great difficulty in expressing his real feelings and so harboured subconscious feelings of aggression and frustration. He subconsciously felt hostile and aggressive to anyone in authority, having had a very bad relationship with his stepmother which had caused him to leave home not long before.

The researchers' assumption was that all this repressed aggression and hostility towards authority had manifested itself in the form of psychokinetic energy, which was the source of the poltergeist activity.

Rapping
A loud series of raps coming from the walls of the house is very typical of poltergeist activity. The raps can get very loud indeed and are often a prelude to a bout of other boisterous poltergeist activity.

Movement of objects
One of the most typical of the phenomena that are associated with poltergeists is the movement of objects in the house. The extent of this movement varies, as does the speed of the movement.

Some objects are hurled at great force across the room to the danger of the inhabitants of the house. Some move slowly, some even virtually in slow motion. The objects sometimes move in a straight line and sometimes adopt a kind of zigzag path.

It is quite common for things to fall off shelves of their own accord. Glasses smash to the floor, as do bottles and sometimes the latter explode.

Teleportation
This is a particular form of movement of objects that is quite common in a household supposedly occupied by a poltergeist. It refers to the moving of objects from one part of the house to another. Sometimes they reappear elsewhere in the house right away but sometimes they

disappear for a while and sometimes they seem to disappear permanently. It is quite common for them to turn up in quite an unexpected place.

Stone-throwing
Another feature of poltergeist activity that has been reported quite regularly through the years is stone-throwing. Most commonly the stones are thrown at the outside walls and roof of the house, a very noisy activity that guarantees that the family in residence get no peace.

At the time that the Perrault family were undergoing their distressing experience it was thought that the poltergeist was some kind of devil. This was still the case slightly later on, early in the eighteenth century, when the house of Samuel Wesley became the focus of poltergeist activity around the end of December 1716 and the beginning of 1717.

Had the existence of a poltergeist been proved it would have been a brave demon indeed, for Samuel Wesley was a clergyman. He was the father of John Wesley who was to become the founder of the Methodist church.

The Fox family and the Rochester Rappings
The theory that a poltergeist was in fact a demon, if in fact it was not a fraud, lasted until about the middle of the nineteenth century when an interest in psychic phenomena increased. This increased interest was partly the result of some poltergeist activity in Hydesville, New York in 1848.

The focus of the poltergeist activity centred on the Fox

family who had just moved house. Not long after they moved in, the two daughters of the family began to hear rapping coming from the walls. Their parents thought that whatever was doing the rapping must have some form of intelligence because if the girls rapped the walls the thing doing the rapping rapped back.

The neighbours got involved and started some sort of primitive communication with the rapper by means of rapping, a kind of code having been devised. One neighbour was amazed that the rapper was able to answer questions about the neighbour's personal life. Later it was thought that the force responsible for this must have acquired the information by some form of telepathy.

The 'Rochester Rappings', as they were known, attracted a large number of people to the house and the conclusion was formed that the rappings and information supposedly supplied through them were emanating from the spirits of dead people. This case is particularly interesting because it led to the founding of a belief in Spiritualism, which rapidly spread through the rest of America and led to a great many people setting up as mediums. Indeed Spiritualism reached almost epidemic proportions.

Later the Fox sisters became professional mediums and were condemned by some as frauds. However, the original rapping on the walls of the Fox family house seems to have been genuine, having been witnessed by many independent, unprejudiced people.

The Fox poltergeist was important in that from then on people tended to think of the poltergeist as the spirit of a dead person rather than as a demon, which they had previously thought. It was important also because the case led to people instigating scientific studies on paranormal or psychic phenomena in America and to the scientific study of poltergeists.

People investigating poltergeists hit a problem that other investigators researching the paranormal also find. This is the fact that you cannot turn paranormal activity on like a tap. When investigators arrived to study the aggressive poltergeist activity reported by the family the poltergeist often did not operate again until the investigators had left. The family members were then left looking as though they had imagined the whole thing or else were suspected of fraud.

The focus of poltergeist activity

Quite early on people interested in poltergeists realized that there was often a connection between the poltergeist and a young person in the house. Before this century this was usually an adolescent girl. Gradually parapsychologists began to suspect that a poltergeist was not in fact a spirit but some kind of product of a human mind, possibly that of the young person who was the focus of the activity.

It was often assumed that poltergeists were the result of some kind of fraud, especially when the poltergeist would not oblige the investigator by making an appearance. Another assumption that was often made was that it was the young person who was perpetrating the fraud to gain attention.

In cases where fraud was ruled out and the focus seemed to be a young person many parapsychologists came to the conclusion that the kind of frenzied activity that the supposed poltergeist was demonstrating, the banging and throwing of things in a seeming tantrum, was akin to some of the behaviour of young people around the age of puberty when their emotions are in a whirl. Anyone who has ever been the parent of someone in his or her early teens will recognize the behaviour pattern—with feeling.

The theory seemed to be that if a child represses the kind of emotions and behaviour that is typical of people around the age of puberty he or she might use psychokinesis unconsciously to find another way of expressing pent-up feelings and frustrations. Thus was born the poltergeist and its often childish acts, so the theory goes.

When modern research did come up with the theory that the mind of a young person in the house could be the cause of the poltergeist activity by means of some kind of psychokinetic process, some researchers began to suspect that there was some kind of sexual element involved simply because the girls involved were all around the age of puberty. They felt that the sexual tensions that were going on inside the girl were responsible for the psychokinetic activity.

Recent research has shown, however, that in Europe and America there has been a change in the age of the people who are commonly the focus of poltergeist activity. The average age when poltergeist activity occurs seems now to be twenty when it was once sixteen. This has to be considered alongside the fact that the age of puberty in Europe and America has generally gone down. Thus puberty and its sexual tensions may not be at the root of poltergeist activity after all.

The other strange change that has happened has already been mentioned above. Poltergeist activity, which usually centred on a young girl or young woman, does not now, in Europe and America, show any form of sexual bias. Cases seem to be equally distributed between females and males. Of course, this need not affect the puberty theory since boys as well as girls are affected by sexual tensions at puberty, except that it was sometimes suggested that poltergeist activity was in some way connected with the onset of the menstrual cycle.

Some researchers have suggested that some form of mental illness might be at the root of the seeming connection between young people and poltergeist activity. Whether or not the child is actually suffering from any sort of mental disorder might be difficult to assess if any relevant examination takes place after the poltergeist activity has begun and the child is in a state of extreme distress. Medical records showing a history of the child before the poltergeist activity began would be more convincing.

Sometimes the factors that subconsciously generate the psychokinesis that leads to poltergeist activity lie in areas other than in puberty or mental illness. It has been described above in the discussion on Julio, given under 'Association with one person', how repressed emotions

can put people in a situation in which poltergeist activity
is a possibility.

Virginia Campbell

It has been seen in the description of the Julio case how
personality and perhaps reaction to life experiences can
affect young people in such a way that researchers feel
could lead to psychokinetic activity of the kind that
could activate a poltergeist. The case of Virginia Campbell
seems to fit the bill.

Virginia was living in the small town of Sauchie in
Scotland with her brother and his wife. In 1960 when
she was eleven the family began to experience poltergeist activity that seemed to be centred on Virginia.

She was going through puberty at the time, but she
was also very unhappy. She had originally lived in Ireland where she was rather lonely, her closest companion
being her pet dog, Toby. Her father decided that he
wanted to live in England, and Virginia was sent to stay
with her brother until things were sorted out.

The poltergeist activity, which included loud banging,
movement and levitation of objects, was bad enough at
home but it followed her to school. A teacher at the school
claimed that Virginia's desk lid tried to rise by itself and
that an unoccupied desk behind her started to levitate.

Virginia was probably unhappy but she was almost
certainly angry at her father because of his decision to
move from her home in Ireland and frustrated at not being able to do anything about it. Her feelings of resent-

ment could not be directed at her parents. Therefore, D. Scott Rogo in his book *The Poltergeist Experience* suggests that, having no one to blame in person and to strike out at, she gave expression to her hostile feelings by psychokinetically giving rise to a poltergeist.

Young people have often been shown to be the focus of poltergeist activity. However, this is not always the case. Now research suggests that an increasing number of elderly people, aged seventy and over, are becoming the focus. However, people need not be at the extremes of age and some researchers have associated poltergeist activity with menopausal women, and this activity has sometimes been known to involve blood.

Winston case

The idea of blood being involved in poltergeist activity is a terrible one for the squeamish. To live through a paranormal experience involving huge amounts of someone else's blood from an unidentifiable source must be a shocking one.

Such a happening is reported to have occurred in Atlanta, Georgia in 1987 when Mr William Winston and his wife found their house splashed with blood and even found some of the floors covered in blood. Both claimed that they had not suffered any loss of blood.

The fact that this was not the blood of either Mr Winston or his wife was borne out by blood analysis. They were both of type A blood and the blood in the house was of type O.

This is a particularly horrible tale. Obviously something very peculiar was going on in the house, and it may have been a poltergeist with a difference. Fortunately this tale is not typical of poltergeist activity generally.

Geophysical solution?

People can speculate about the cause of poltergeist activity and put it down to some kind of psychokinesis but no one really knows what causes it. It has been suggested, in particular by Guy Lambert, that there is a rational cause behind supposed poltergeist activity and that it is caused geophysically.

He argued that underground water channels might create an effect similar to poltergeist activity if they ran below or very close to the foundations of buildings.When a head of water has built up in any of these channels, the building might be subject to spasmodic upward thrusts. These thrusts, he argued, might create noises in the building over the channels that could be taken for rapping and might also be strong enough to cause movement of objects in rooms.

People have counter-argued that, if this were the case, floods and high tides would be likely to make for an increase in the incidence of the disturbances of the kind caused by poltergeist activity. This has not been found to be the case.

Lambert argued that poltergeist activity was greater in coastal and tidal areas than elsewhere, supposedly pointing to the truth of his theory. However, it was pointed out that these areas tend to have the highest densities of population

In addition two researchers, Dr Alan Gauld, a psychologist from Nottingham University, and Tony Cornell, who had much experience in poltergeist research, acquired for their research purposes some terraced houses which were scheduled for demolition that, although they were structurally quite sound. They brought in equipment that produced physical force that was much higher in intensity than that which would have been caused by water channels.

Very strong vibrations were produced in the houses, yet no movement of objects of the kind supposedly caused by poltergeists was witnessed. It seemed as though the poltergeist had lived to fight another day

Summary

As is the case with much paranormal activity, the truth about poltergeists is that we are not yet sure what gives rise to them. The typical happenings associated with them have been fairly well documented and various theories have been put forward as to their cause.

These have changed over the years. We have gone from demons, to spirits of the dead, to sexually confused adolescent children, to anyone in a state of repressed aggression and hostility. For the moment at least it seems agreed that the mind seems once again to be exerting its power over our lives to the extent of causing much distress and discomfort in the form of poltergeists.

Chapter 2

Telepathy

Throughout history there have been many reports of events and many claims of occurrences that involve the mind and cannot be explained in terms of the accepted theories, especially scientific theories, of the time. Such events are usually classified as 'paranormal', rather a vague term variously defined as 'beyond the normal', 'abnormal' or 'not explicable by the laws of nature or reason'.

As these definitions would suggest, paranormal is rather a loose term. Under its umbrella can come a rag-bag collection of just about anything that seems beyond the comprehension of our usual senses. Telepathy is one of these.

Telepathy is a branch of ESP or extrasensory perception, the alleged ability to acquire information about people, events or objects at some place or time that is distant to the present by some means that is not yet known to science. There are several aspects of the paranormal that can be categorized under ESP but telepathy is the only one that involves person-to-person ESP.

The word 'telepathy' according to *Chambers English Dictionary* means 'communication between mind and mind otherwise than through the known channels of the senses'. In other words the mind would once again appear to be exerting a good deal of power, and a power that we do not understand.

Scepticism

There is much scepticism about telepathy, as there is indeed about anything connected with ESP or the paranormal in general. Certainly there are a number of things to be taken into consideration before one gives any credence to the many reported and anecdotal accounts of ESP or telepathy.

The first thing to be taken into consideration is that the human memory cannot be relied on because it is essentially fallible. Things that people report as true may contain a germ of truth but at best may be remembered imperfectly and at worse may be subjected to a good deal of exaggeration, embroidery or even untruth.

The second is that most of us, however cynical we may pride ourselves on being, tend to be suggestible. We are capable of seeing things that are not there if we want to see them enough or if someone suggests that we ought to be able to see them. If everyone says that they are experiencing something paranormal why should we not?

Then we have, unfortunately, to take fraud into consideration. This is unlikely in an anecdotal account by an ordinary member of the public. Such a person might mislead but would not be likely to perpetrate a fraud. However, the possibility of fraud relating to stage acts or the media cannot be ruled out, although some of these might be more correctly called hoaxes.

In the case of supposed telepathy there is also the predictability factor to be taken into consideration when one is wondering how much credence to give to a reported account of a telepathic incident. Of course it is extremely difficult to decide what is a predictable event and what is not. There is often a fine line to be drawn between these.

Predictability factor

An extreme case will serve to demonstrate the potential predictability factor. If someone seems to receive ESP information about the death of a relative, whether he or she seems just to receive some form of message that leads to a certainty of death or actually seems to see an apparition, the age and circumstances of the relative should be taken into consideration.

Should the said relative be a young, healthy person in the peak of condition, both physically and mentally, the seeming ESP or telepathic information would be considerably more surprising and less predictable than it would be if the relative involved was a very old, frail person who has for several months been suffering from a terminal condition and who has been thought to be at death's door for several weeks. A feeling, message or apparition would be pretty surprising in any circumstances but less so if the subject of the message was expected to die in the near future and the recipient of the supposed mes-

sage knew this. The now dead relative would have probably been on the mind of the recipient of the ESP information already.

Personality

Also to be taken into consideration to some extent is the
personality of the alleged recipient of the message.
Someone who is extremely anxious and constantly worries that the members of her close family are away from
her, imagining that danger and disaster are around every
corner waiting to beset them, is less likely to be taken seriously if she has some kind of reported telepathic experience than someone who is more carefree or laid back.
She may claim to have felt that something terrible had
happened to her daughter when it actually had, but she
may have felt that way every night—and possibly most
of the day—without anything untoward happening.

Card-testing

Tests have been devised to try and assess the feasibility
of telepathy. An early test was a card-testing experiment
using a special five-card deck. It was developed by
Joseph Banks Rhine who began the modern interest in
parapsychology, and in ESP particularly, while working
at Duke University in North Carolina in the 1930s.

His subjects in the original test had to guess the sequence of cards that would occur, the cards being shuf-
fled thoroughly to make sure that they were in a random
and therefore unpredictable order, thereby hoping to ex-

clude the possibility of the subjects guessing correctly by logical inference. The results showed that a good many of the subjects were able to predict the card sequence correctly more frequently than would be expected by chance.

Some investigators have been sceptical about Rhine's findings. It was felt by some that Rhine and his workers were so anxious to prove the existence of ESP and telepathy that they may have unconsciously influenced the subjects in their choice of cards, for example by unconsciously giving them some subtle hints or cues. The fact that they could not reproduce Rhine's results in their own laboratories also made other investigators sceptical.

Stepanek

However, a Czech researcher, Milan Ryzl, at the beginning of the 1960s began experimenting with hypnosis to try to train or strengthen people in extrasensory abilities such as telepathy. In the course of his research Ryzl encountered a man called Pavel Stepanek who did not prove to be a good subject for hypnosis but who began to show quite extraordinary levels of ESP in Ryzl's experiments, again based on the card-choosing theme, and then in experiments with a range of other researchers. Even here there were some sceptics, but it was widely recognized that mere chance could not account for Stepanek's scores in experiments conducted by numerous researchers.

So much for academic research. Meanwhile most ordinary people have their own opinion of ESP and telepathy. Some dismiss the whole thing without another thought, while others believe in some form of transference of information other than by the ordinary means and others are not sure. Surveys show that most have some belief.

One difficulty about trying to prove the viability or otherwise of someone's telepathic abilities is that people seem rarely to be able to call on the gift to order. George Gilbert Murray (1866–1957), a well-known Greek scholar, used to try to demonstrate his telepathic ability and to try to improve on it by playing some kind of guessing games with his family. The results of fifty years, playing of these games were published by the Society for Psychical Research. It emerged that Murray achieved accuracy in about one third of his guesses.

It would appear that most scientists, according to surveys, do not believe in ESP or telepathy. Perhaps this is because their very training teaches them to believe only what can be proved conclusively, and it is difficult to do this with telepathy. Besides, all paranormal phenomena almost by definition seem to break the known laws of science and of nature. It is thought, however, that more scientists than before seem prepared to keep a more open mind, although doubtless some of them may still be too prejudiced even to do that.

Mind-reading

Stage shows have done much to discredit ESP and telepathy. Many people are convinced that the performer tries to pull the wool over the eyes of the members of the audience or the viewers by a series of tricks. They feel that he or she might have done some kind of preliminary research on the lives of the people whom they plan to interview so that their revelations will appear extraordinary and even paranormal. Alternatively, they feel that the performer who is going to do the 'mind-reading' may have colleagues who make a practice of circulating among the group containing the intended subjects so that they may find out something about them and their lives, which they will report back to the 'mind-reader' before he embarks on his performance.

There may be some truth in this scepticism. Certainly most performers, such as stage magicians, who wish to impress audiences with their supposed paranormal skills have a few tricks up their sleeves. Even if they had the gift of telepathy they would not be able to demonstrate it all of the time. Telepathy, like other forms of extrasensory perception, seems to be inconsistent in its application. Whether or not a particular performer has any telepathic power, it is unfortunately true that the misgivings that have become attached to stage 'mind-readers' have affected some people's perception about telepathy generally. Yet there have been some remarkable reported cases of telepathy.

The word is said to have been coined by Frederick Myers, an inspector of schools, a poet and one of the founders of the Society for Psychical Research, established in 1882. He defined it as 'the communication of impressions of any kind from one mind to another independently of the recognized channels of the senses.'

Donne

Many reported examples of telepathy relate to some kind of crisis or disaster. An early example predates Myers by several hundred years and concerns the poet John Donne (1572–1631). According to Sir Izaak Walton, the poet had an experience of what was later to be called telepathy when he was on a diplomatic mission to France in 1610. When he arrived in France he told the English ambassador that he had seen a terrible vision of his wife, who had stayed at home in England, being pregnant at the time.

Donne claimed that he had twice seen his wife pass by him in the room with her hair hanging around her shoulders and holding a dead baby in her arms. Sir Robert Drury, the English ambassador, was rather sceptical but agreed to send a messenger to Donne's home in England to ascertain if there was anything the matter with his wife.

Nearly two weeks later the messenger returned to Donne in France with the news that his wife had been very ill and unhappy, having had a long labour that had resulted in her giving birth to a dead baby. After some investigation it was discovered that the time at which Donne had claimed to see the vision of his wife with the dead baby was the very time that she was delivered of the stillborn child.

Cassirer

Another recorded example of supposed telepathic responses to crises relates to Ernst Cassirer who was professor of philosophy at the university of Hamburg from 1919 until Hitler came to power in 1933. He seems to have been unduly sensitive to the state of his daughter's health when she was away from him.

Anna Cassirer has spoken of her father ringing her up at her boarding school in the middle of the night on several occasions because he had a feeling that there was something wrong with her. On each of these occasions Anna was ill and in the school sick bay. This kind of night-time call was extremely unusual and he never made one when his daughter was quite well.

Anna tells a similar story about a time when her father visited her when she was a student in Berlin. After they had been at an evening party together, Cassirer left the next morning by train to return to Hamburg but got out at the only place that the express train stopped before then. He telephoned his daughter at her lodgings because he had had a sudden feeling that there was something very far wrong with her and was told that she had been taken to hospital. On contacting the hospital he was told that she had been admitted with a haemorrhage that had begun shortly after his train left the station.

These then are examples of supposed telepathy that have been officially reported—in the case of Donne by his biographer and in the case of Cassirer by his daughter to a psychical researcher. However, I am sure that in the course of our everyday lives most of us have come across anecdotal accounts, whether told directly to us or told at second or third hand, in which people have claimed to have had some telepathic message, vision or feeling about some kind of misfortune in the life of someone else, often someone close to them.

Examples of telepathy

The misfortune need not be a particularly tragic one— indeed it can be relatively trivial. For example, I know of one mother who seemed to have an uncanny knack of appearing at her children's primary school just as it was about to close very early for some reason or other so that she could collect her children. This early closing was unusual, happening only in response to some relatively rare crisis. The crises were not only rare but varied—and so it would not really have been possible for the mother to predict a crisis.

One time it was a bad snow storm in the part of the town where the school was, although not in the part of the town where the mother worked. Another time it was a complete breakdown of the central heating system and on another occasion it was a minor fire, the events taking place over the six years or so of the children's attendance. She never appeared early if there was no sudden early closing and no one had ever contacted her in advance.

When queried about her unusual ability to appear in response to a school crisis in this way she said that she just knew that there was something wrong and left work to drive to the school. She did not even stop to telephone to verify her concern.

Other anecdotal accounts of supposed telepathy are more serious or more tragic, perhaps because examples of ESP in this area tend to stick in people's memories. Something less dramatic might quite easily slip people's minds.

It is common to hear of people who have woken in the middle of the night convinced that someone close to them has had a terrible accident only to find either then or the next morning that this is in fact the case and that a close relative or friend has been badly injured. People in these circumstances sometimes think that they saw an apparition of the injured person, others do not.

For example, a mother whose daughter was living in America at the time had gone to bed relatively early only to wake in terror around midnight convinced that her daughter was in great danger. The terror was followed almost immediately by a great sense of relief.

She rang her daughter but she was not at home, although she should have returned from work by then— there is of course a time difference between Britain and America. The mother left a message for her daughter to ring her as soon as she could, even though in Britain it was now the middle of the night.

When the daughter did so it was to tell her mother that she and a group of friends had been standing at the corner of a street when a car came hurtling towards them at enormous speed. They were in great danger and tried to leap out of the way. The girl in question did so safely, although one of her friends was tragically killed.

It is of course impossible to test the veracity of this anecdote, even if one knows both parties involved. Suffice to say that both mother and daughter are exceptionally practical people who had never had such an experience before. The mother was used to having her daughter travel the world and was not the neurotic sort who spent all her time worrying about what might be happening to her.

Another mother speaks of sitting at home late one afternoon waiting for her primary-school-age son to come home from school by the school bus. Suddenly she was gripped by the most terrible feeling that her son was in a dangerous situation. She rushed to get her car and drove along the short route that she knew the school bus took. When she saw the bus not far along the route from the school she flagged it down, only to discover that her son was not on it and that none of his friends seemed to know why.

Thoroughly alarmed, she got back into the car and raced to the school. Just by the telephone box near the school gates she saw her son. He was standing talking to a man who ran off when he saw the mother coming towards them.

The son seemed very upset, and it was some time before he was able to speak about what had happened in a reasonably calm manner. When he did so he spoke of the fact that a teacher had held him back by asking him to run a small errand, not realizing that this would make the boy miss his bus home.

On finding out that the bus had just left without him he went towards the phone box near the school gates to make a reverse charge call home and explain the situation. Just as he reached it a man came up to him and asked him what the matter was. He told the boy not to worry his mother, whom he said he knew, that he had his car nearby and would run the boy home.

It was just at that point that the boy's mother drove up and all was well. The boy did say that, although he kept telling the man that he had been told not to accept lifts from strangers, the man was very persuasive and kept telling him that he was a family friend, which he was not, and that the stranger ban then did not apply to him.

This account of supposed telepathy had a happy outcome for the family of the person claiming to have experienced the ESP, but this is not true for everyone. A few months after this incident a boy was abducted from near the school gates and was badly beaten up and sexually abused.

Not all accounts by ordinary people of supposed telepathy end happily, even for the people most closely concerned. A wife whose husband was a salesman and was away on a business trip speaks of how, very early one morning, she had a sudden picture of him surrounded by flames and screaming out in terror.

She could not get hold him of him, but this was by no

means unusual when he was away as his business plans were often subject to sudden change. The only fire she could find reported was a fatal fire in a private house in a town that was miles away from where he was meant to be and in any case he was staying in a hotel.

At this she began to relax although it turned that she had little cause to do so. It was in fact her husband who had been killed. Having talked to his sales manager the pattern of his journey had changed. He was to join a fellow salesman in the latter's own town with a view to making a particularly strong sales pitch for their product against a new competitor.

Time was pressing and he set off without telling his wife of the change of plan, intending to ring her next morning. He was persuaded by his sales colleague to spend the night with him and his family rather than go to a hotel. Unfortunately a fire broke out in the house and, although the family members were saved, their guest died in the blaze.

It is difficult to know what to make of accounts like this. In this particular case, friends testified to the fact that the woman who claimed to have had the telepathic experience was far from being a specially imaginative person and that she was so used to having her husband travelling around the country a great deal of the time that she never worried unnecessarily about him.

In cases like the one just described it is important, if any credence is to be attached to it, that there has been some evidence that the person claiming to have had the telepathic experience has told several people about the experience before the actual tragedy was revealed. Otherwise the whole episode could easily have become confused in the mind of someone suffering from great grief. On the other hand, if someone does have such a very vivid suggestion that a member of the family is in danger, he or she is not likely to hang about telling people about it but will rush around trying to find out if the relative is all right.

Another case of supposed telepathy experienced by quite ordinary people relates to a woman who is now in her fifties. She still claims to have a very vivid recollection about a telepathic experience that she claims to have experienced about thirty years ago when she was a young woman.

According to her, she woke for no seeming reason in the middle of the night and saw an apparition of her father lying with his eyes closed and looking very pale. She experienced a great feeling of doom and was convinced that he was dead rather than just sleeping.

She leapt out of bed and went to ring her father who lived at the other side of the country, hoping to set her mind at rest. Her father lived alone and when she did not get a reply she phoned his next-door neighbour, although she realized that calling in the middle of the night was a distinctly antisocial experience if nothing was wrong.

His neighbours knew him very well and said that he had not told them of any plans to be away from home, which he usually did. They were sufficiently concerned about what their neighbour's daughter told them that they rang him themselves. On receiving no reply they went round and rang the doorbell but again received no response.

They had a key for emergencies and duly used this to gain entry. They looked around the house and found their neighbour dead in bed. Later investigations revealed that he had died of a heart condition that had been undiagnosed in his lifetime.

At this time the woman who claimed to have had the telepathic experience was in her early twenties and her father was only in his early forties. Thus it was not likely that he would die and there would have been no reason for her to be worrying about his health. Also neither she nor he had known of his heart condition.

Accounts like this, which involve other people, are difficult to refute. However, often by the time one actually hears the account either from the person who claims to have experienced the telepathic experience or from some of the other people, the actual time of the experience is long past and the people involved either far apart from each other or dead. It is thus difficult to check up on such situations.

It is this kind of account that tends to get handed on from one member of a family to another to become in time part of the family folk history. There may often be a germ of truth in the original story but it has got embroidered over the years.

Pain

Pain is sometimes involved in claimed telepathic accounts. For example, a man whose brother had his right arm severed at the elbow claims to have experienced a searing pain in the area around the elbow of his right arm at the very time that he later discovered his brother had had his terrible accident.

Another man spoke of sitting at his desk in his office when he suddenly experienced a searing pain in his ankle and thoughts of his younger brother entered his mind. The pain was almost intolerable according to his account and he later discovered that it had occurred at the time of day that his brother had had his foot severed in a terrible multiple car crash on a motorway.

It is again difficult to submit such accounts to any rigorous testing, especially if they come to light some time after the actual incident. That is why it is difficult for scientists to give very much credence to such accounts in the debate about whether or not there is such a thing as telepathy or ESP. On the other hand, there are so many accounts that relate claimed telepathic experiences that it is difficult not to believe that there is nothing in it at all.

Boughey

Sometimes there appears to be some kind of concrete evidence to back up a claimed telepathic experience. That would appear to have been so in the case relating to Leslie Boughey, a case researched for the television series, Arthur C. Clarke's World of Mysterious Powers.

In this case of claimed telepathy Leslie Boughey was stationed with the RAF in Egypt in 1947 when he woke one night with an agonizing pain in his hand with the pain centring on one finger in particular. There was no obvious reason for the pain. No mark, swelling or any sign of injury or infection was to be seen. Yet the pain was very great and subsided only after a considerable time.

Boughey and his wife in England were in the habit of writing to each other every day, as was frequently the case in those days when a member of the Services was overseas, and tended to mention most things relating to their daily lives. This being the case, Boughey duly reported to his wife his distressing and painful experience with his finger.

Meanwhile his wife was writing to him to tell him about an incident that had happened to her in the factory where she worked. Apparently a small piece of metal penetrated her finger and became embedded in it. The wound was extremely painful. It went septic and had to be lanced by the doctor causing much pain for a time before the finger began to heal.

Her letter telling her husband of this apparently crossed with his letter to her telling her of his strange experience. They discovered that the time of her operation coincided with the time of his strange painful experience and his unaccounted-for pain was on the same finger of the same hand.

This was a strange tale and presumably could have been given some credence by the letters. These would have been a kind of concrete evidence but whether they were kept or not, whether indeed they are still in existence or not, I do not know.

One of the interesting things about this case is that the circumstances were not tragic in any way and did not really amount to a crisis. Doubtless Boughey's wife's finger was extremely painful but she was in no actual danger. She probably mentioned it to her husband simply because she wrote everyday and was used to telling him all about what happened to her. If you write to someone every day you make good use of any event The same is true of her husband. In other circumstances he might not have bothered mentioning this strange happening.

Thus it is possible that there are more supposed telepathic experiences regarding fairly minor pain than we actually hear of. We are much more likely to hear of more dramatic occurrences, especially those involving great injury or death.

Relatives sometimes refer to supposed telepathic experiences they have had when people close to them are experiencing surgery, although often they did not know about this surgery in advance. One friend of mind tells of the time when out of the blue one afternoon she began to experience the most excruciatingly sharp pain in her back.

She knew that her father was in hospital for diagnostic tests for back pain, but she had no idea that he was having surgery to try to cure the problem. There had been no question of that when she last visited him or when she had last spoken to her mother. It transpired that the decision to operate had been taken by the surgeon quite recently and that her mother was keeping the fact from her daughter so as not to worry her since she was about to sit her final university exams.

Twins and telepathy

Twins, especially identical twins, are known to have a special relationship. Although there is no actual proof that twins have ESP or that they communicate by telepathy, however, it is generally admitted that twins do seem to have a heightened sense of empathy and are exceptionally sensitive to each other's thoughts and feelings, and some of the anecdotes that circulate about the experience of twins certainly resemble some that relate to other people's claimed telepathic experiences.

A woman who had an identical twin claimed to have one day felt a sensation of tremendous heat and pain and then experienced a black void. She soon discovered that her twin had been killed in a plane crash at that very time.

A less tragic story centres on a man who was suffering from terrible toothache in one of his top back teeth one day. He got an emergency appointment with a dentist, so painful was the tooth, but the dentist could find nothing wrong with it and concluded that the pain must be a result of sinusitis. The pain quite suddenly went away shortly afterwards and later that day he heard from his twin who lived in the next town that he had had to have one of his top back teeth extracted that day. It was the same tooth.

There are many anecdotes concerning twins and pregnancy. It is by no means uncommon for a twin to claim to feel labour pains when her sister, currently at some distance from her, has actually gone into labour. Obviously the non-pregnant twin would have known that her pregnant twin was actually pregnant and she could probably relatively easily predict roughly the date of the delivery but accounts of claimed telepathic experiences like this occur in cases when the birth was premature and the other twin could not have predicted the time of labour.

The kind of heightened empathy that exists between twins sometimes seems to exist, although probably to a lesser degree, between other people. The kind of claimed sympathetic labour pains mentioned above in the case of twins are sometimes claimed to be experienced by a husband when he is at a distance from his wife when she gives birth. Again, it could be argued that he could have predicted the approximate time of birth, but anecdotes exist about husbands who had pains when their wives went into early labour or were having a miscarriage.

Some kind of ability to communicate with each other on a level other than through the ordinary five senses is not all that surprising between twins given the unusual nature of their relationship. However, there are reported cases of claimed telepathic experiences occurring when the person who underwent the experience did not know the other person involved very well and certainly did not have strong emotional ties with him or her.

Casas

One of these concerns an old Spanish woman called Isabella Casas. Reuben Stone describes in his book *Mysteries of the Mind* how one morning in 1980 she went to her local police station in Barcelona and told the police that she had just had a terrible dream about one of her neighbours. In the dream he was terrified and told her that someone was going to kill them.

She usually saw her neighbour, a chef called Rafael Perez, every day but she had not seen him for some time, about ten days or so. Unusually she had had a note delivered to her by hand from him a few days after she had last seen him saying that he would be away from home for several weeks. This she thought was unusual but then it is not so unusual for people to be called away for some reason or other.

Probably partly because the old woman was so upset the police decided to look into the matter and went to Perez' apartment. They found him eventually tied up in the utility room on the roof of the apartment house in which he and Isabella Casas lived. He had been left like that by burglars who had stolen his cheque book and made him write out cheques to them for all his savings.

They had said that when they had cashed all the cheques and acquired all the money they would return and kill him and the old lady but when they did return the police arrested them.

Admittedly the situation was very urgent and it was one that involved Isabella's own life. Still, although she and Perez were quite friendly as neighbours they had no blood ties and no real emotional ties.

Primitive telepathy

There are those who feel that telepathy is a natural part of life but that the nature of western life is that we have lost the gift for it. They claim that many simpler peoples with a more primitive, more natural way of life may still retain the gift to a far greater extent than we in the west.

Certainly there are various accounts of telepathic experiences witnessed by travellers who have visited primitive tribespeople. For example, Richard St Barbe Baker, in his memoirs, *African Drums*, published in the 1930s, wrote of the telepathic communication that seemed to exist among the Kenyan tribespeople whom he met while conservator of forests in Kenya.

In his book Baker tells of an old tribesman saying that he knows of the death of a local farmer who lived more than two hundred miles away because he had just seen him dying. Everyone else assumed that the farmer was still alive until seven days later when they received the news that the farmer had died just about the time that the tribesman had claimed to have seen it.

Some people think that telepathy may be an ability that we have lost as our society has become more and more sophisticated and industrialized. They believe that, as we have moved away from a more simple, primitive way of life, where we had to rely more on our selves and on our own initiative, any telepathic powers that we would have had naturally have become blocked.

Summary
The subject of telepathy is a fascinating one. Although published reported cases are rare many of us have come into contact with alleged anecdotal experiences in some way in the course of our lives. Many of us would like to know more about it. The scientists would like to know how it works, if it indeed exists.

However, the mind-to-mind direct transference of information that makes up telepathy remains a mystery. Science may one day throw some light on the subject, as it has a habit of doing. Perhaps it will always remain a mystery. It may be that in telepathy the mind is reminding us that it is in charge of the other senses.

Chapter 3

Precognition

Precognition, like telepathy, is a branch of ESP, or extra-sensory perception, in that it relies on ESP to detect information about future events. I say *is* a branch of ESP, although many people would dispute the fact that there is any such thing as precognition, or predicting the future (literally foreknowledge), or ESP. Perhaps it would be safer to say that precognition, if there were such a phenomenon, would be a branch of ESP if it exists.

We have seen in the previous chapter on Telepathy how many people, particularly scientists, are sceptical about the existence of telepathy. This is nothing, however, compared with the degree of scepticism about precognition.

Most people would probably not be familiar with the word 'precognition', but they would be familiar with the supposed concept of predicting future events. Perhaps precognition is one of the most interesting and disturbing of the mind's claimed paranormal abilities. That the human mind can make nonsense of time scales is an awesome thought.

Unfortunately the phrase 'predicting future events' suggests 'fortune-telling' to many people. This phrase often has unfortunate connotations for many of us.

Fortune-telling

This in turn conjures up to many of us pictures of one of the village residents dressed up in headscarf and curtain-ring earrings, possibly with a fake tan added for a more convincing effect, sitting in a tent at the village fair, looking into a glass ball and pretending to be a gypsy who is ready to tell people's future if they will cross her hand with silver, the said silver being destined for some worthy charity. Actually a village resident of relatively long standing might make quite a good job of predicting the likely futures of some of those other residents whose pasts she knew well.

Alternatively it brings to mind someone peering into a teacup in order to see if the tea leaves reveal anything resembling a tall dark stranger or a journey over water. Attempts to predict the future by reading the tea leaves may have decreased when most people turned to the tea bag but they still exist.

Crystal-ball reading

Although we tend to think of the crystal ball as essentially being part of the apparatus of the fair-ground fortune-teller described above, divination by means of a crystal ball is still quite common. Nowadays, the so-called crystal ball is often made of clear glass rather than rock crystal or beryl, as they used to be.

People who claim to be able to see the future by means of crystal balls are sometimes called scryers. Some scryers claim that, when they first gaze into it, the crystal or glass ball becomes cloudy and that, as it clears, images appear that enable them to interpret the future.

These images are often just cloudy masses of an indistinct shape, the colour of these being important. For example, white clouds suggest good fortune, black clouds suggest evil, green suggests hope, and so on.

Some scryers claim to be able to see more than just cloudy masses. They claim to be able to see actual shapes and even whole scenes from the future.

Astrology
The point is that to a lot of us fortune-telling is a bit of a joke, maybe an enjoyable joke but certainly not something that we would admit to taking seriously. We may rush to read our horoscopes in the paper every day—which self-respecting tabloid would be without a tame astrologer?—but we rarely believe the prediction given for the day, and few of us would alter our plans for the day in the light of what was said.

By no means does everyone regard astrology in this light. According to some professional astrologers there has been a marked increase in the number of people making appointments for a consultation so that they can see what the future holds. I suppose it is possible that if the present appears bleak, with a rash of redundancies, unemployment, mounting debt, negative equity and repossessed houses, then all some people can do is place their faith in the future, and who can blame them for wanting to take a little premature peek.

In any case, many people hope to get more out of astrology than predictions about their future lives. Many hope to use astrology to get a greater insight into their real selves and possibly to receive help to achieve their true potential. Still, for most of us astrology remains something to be taken lightly.

Palmistry

Palmistry is another method that some people use to try to predict someone's future, although many reputable people who are engaged in palmistry are at pains to point out that people engaged in palmistry do not actually predict the future by studying someone's palm but simply indicate tendencies or possibilities that might occur in his or her life. By studying the palm they are also able to reveal things about the personality and life of the person whose hand is being read.

The art of palmistry involves studying the shape, size and general appearance of the hand, including the fingers, and the length, thickness and positioning of the thumb. It also involves studying the slightly raised areas of the palm, known as mounts, such as Jupiter, Venus and Mars. Both major and minor lines on the hand are also part of the study.

The major lines include the heart line, which indicates emotional feeling, the head line, which indicates mental faculties and intelligence, and the life line, which indicates physical wellbeing. The minor lines, which are not present on all palms, include the line of fate, the line of

fortune, also known as the line of success, and the line of
health.

Anyone thinking of taking up palmistry, whether as a
hobby or as a profession, should not hope to grasp the
subject quickly. It is a complex subject, not least because the lines on a palm are rarely as clearly delineated
and etched as illustrations of palms in books of palmistry suggest.

Card-readings

Some people who wish to take a look into the future turn
to card-readers. There are card-readers who claim to be
able to tell fortunes by means of a pack of ordinary playing cards, certain cards being supposed to have certain
meanings or to suggest certain events. For example, the
nine of spades is said to indicate bad luck, loss and con-
flict, the eight of diamonds is supposed to indicate a
pleasant journey or a late marriage, and the ten of
hearts joy, love, good fortune and the realization of am-
bition.

Other card-readers do not use ordinary playing cards
but use tarot cards instead. Tarot card-reading, having
been out of favour for quite a while, is enjoying a new
popularity.

The standard tarot pack consists of 78 cards, which are
completely different from playing cards. Again, various
meanings are assigned to various cards, and these are in-
terpreted by the tarot card-reader for the person seeking
help. Tarot card-reading is a more complicated proce-

dure than the reading of playing cards. There is held to be a spiritual aspect to tarot cards, although this is not now emphasized as much as it once was

Clairvoyants

The word 'clairvoyant' is often used with the same meaning as fortune-teller in the sense that we have just been discussing. Thus someone might speak of going to see a clairvoyant to have the tarot cards read. It is also used to describe someone who claims to have precognitive experiences, such as someone who has had a vision of a future disaster. In addition, the word is also sometimes used of someone who claims generally to have psychic powers.

The derivation of the word does not help. It is derived from a French word that is in turn derived from French *clair*, 'clear', and French *voir*, 'to see'.

However, in ESP studies it is usually used to mean the detection of information about objects or events by some sense other than the five normal senses, in other words, by ESP. It is used in this sense in this book and it is dealt with in Chapter 4.

There are many people engaged in the various forms of fortune-telling. Some of them are professionals, some of them are enthusiastic amateurs who are simply trying their supposed skills on their friends or who are simply having a bit of a laugh.

The people who consult professional fortune-tellers probably divide into two groups. One group are prob-

ably going partly out of interest and partly out of curios-
ity. They will most likely be approaching the experience
with at least some degree of scepticism and probably
with a good deal of ambivalence. The other group are
probably going with a greater sense of belief and very
possibly a sense of desperation, having failed to find any
other kind of help.

It is, of course, impossible to decide how many, or if
indeed any, of the people who claim to be able to predict
the future of others and who set about trying to do so
as a profession have any form of psychic power, or if
indeed there is such a thing as psychic power. Doubtless
there are a good many frauds among them and doubtless
there are some of them who really feel that they have
a gift.

The people who consult them are more important. If
they are in a vulnerable state they are likely to be gulli-
ble and to be inclined to believe everything they hear.
What is important is that people, particularly those in a
vulnerable state, are not told anything that will cause
them further distress. In particular they should not be
told anything suggesting that they have not much longer
to live or that they are dangerously ill.

If no one is actually damaged by the experience of
consulting someone who claims to be able to predict the
future and if no excessive fees are charged then not
much harm is done. Some good may even be done if
someone is given hope for the future.

This, however, raises the question of how accurate the

predictions of self-styled fortune-tellers are. Only the
people who consult them are in a position to know and
even then it might be years before they are in a position
to make any kind of judgement.

Even if fortune-tellers do predict something that turns
out to be accurate it does not necessarily mean that they
have any kind of paranormal power. For a start there is
the role played by coincidence.

Then there is the role played by predictability. People
claiming to be fortune-tellers can get quite a lot of information out of the clients by subtle, skilful questioning of
which the client may be quite unaware. This together
with reasonable powers of observation, which can tell a
great deal about the client's circumstances, can help the
supposed fortune-teller predict with some degree of accuracy, and without any degree of paranormal power, a
few things that might be likely to happen to the client.
The said powers of observation can help the fortune-
teller deduce a lot about the client from his or her appearance, age, sex, speech, clothes, etc, in the way that a
detective might do.

Naturally there is also the attitude of the client. If people have a deep belief in the powers of the fortune-teller
they may well interpret what happens in their lives later
as having fulfilled a prophecy whether or not this is actually the case. In addition, some supposed fortune-tellers are exceptionally clever in making rather loose, very
wide statements that might fit any number of future
situations.

Then, of course, there are all the predictions that are made by supposed fortune-tellers that never come anywhere near to coming true. These tend to be swept under the carpet and forgotten about. Only the seemingly sensational is remembered.

So much for professional or amateur 'fortune-tellers', but there do seem to be people who seem to have a strange gift that could be described as the gift of prophecy. We have had such people throughout history and we still have them in the twentieth century.

Prediction and premonition

As with other forms of the paranormal or ESP there is a good deal of scepticism attached to precognition. It is difficult to put one's credence in someone's ability to have foreknowledge of future events, but there have been various reported examples of this, which are difficult to refute.

Major disasters seem to attract precognition or claims of precognition. Many people claim to have successfully predicted terrible disaster of some kind and several of these claims have been reported in print. Some of the disasters are of national or international proportions and some are more of a local or domestic nature.

Scepticism

There are those who claim that precognition or premonition, a feeling that something is going to happen, and often more or less amounting to the same thing as precognition, cannot exist. They say that precognition is just an example of someone claiming after an event that they knew about the event beforehand. It is not, however, as simple as that as there are recorded cases where the prediction has been noted before the event took place.

Some people claim that many of the predictions and premonitions that people claim to have are usually of a vague or nonspecific nature. Someone may have a premonition that a plane will crash, without being very specific as to exact time and place. Given the number of planes that regularly travel the skies, those claiming such an example of supposed precognition are almost certain to be proved right on the basis of statistics alone.

Doubtless there are examples of this but to damn all examples of precognition in this way is decidedly unfair. Many people who do predict disasters are not totally nonspecific and some of them, particularly when members of their family or friends are involved, are very specific indeed.

Aberfan

A modern documented case of precognition of disaster was not absolutely specific in that the prediction does not appear to have named the actual place. On the other hand, the level of detail given was such that it had to give the most hardened sceptic something to think about.

The disaster occurred at Aberfan, a mining village in

South Wales. On 21 October at 9.15 a.m. in 1966 the coal tip by the village slid in avalanche proportions down towards the village and swamped it. One of the most tragic aspects of the disaster was the number of children who were killed.

Pantglas Junior School was right in the path of the black avalanche and it was covered by it. Given the time of day, the children were in school and over a hundred of them were killed as well as many adults. It was a tragedy of cataclysmic proportions and one that was unbearably poignant because of the number of children that were involved.

Obviously there were many newspaper reports after the incident, such a horrific disaster having caught the attention of the world's press as well as the nation's. What was more disturbing was the fact that there were several well-documented accounts of the disaster before it happened, although the actual place was not mentioned.

Perhaps the most famous of these was a prediction made by a woman at a Spiritualist church in Plymouth on the evening of 20 October. In the presence of six witnesses she told how she had had a vision in which an avalanche of coal hurtled down a hill towards a terrified child at the bottom. She also spoke of seeing an old schoolhouse and a Welsh miner. The morning of the disaster at around 8.30 the same woman told a neighbour about her vision.

This kind of prediction is difficult to ignore. Admittedly the woman was not specific about the place but the disaster was very unusual. Had it been an avalanche of snow that was involved there would have been more cause for scepticism but avalanches of coal are distinctly rarer.

Furthermore the woman in Plymouth was not the only person who made a prediction concerning the Aberfan disaster. One of the children in Aberfan is said to have told her parents some time before the disaster that she had dreamt that she went to school as usual only to find that the school was not there, that it was covered all over in something black. This account was not only verified by the child's parents but by the local minister.

A woman in Sidcup in Kent also claimed to have had a dream about a disaster in a coal-mining village. This dream occurred seven days before the Aberfan disaster and two friends confirmed, one of them in writing, that she had told them about her dream four days before it happened. She apparently had spoken of seeing a building filled with children and coal and water rushing towards the building and burying it. She also spoke of the screams of the children.

Titanic

The sinking of the *Titanic* was a major disaster and one that also attracted a great many claimed predictions. The British liner on a voyage to America sank on the night of 14–15 April 1912 after striking an iceberg. It was the ship's maiden voyage. More than 1500 of the 2200 people aboard died in the disaster, partly, it was said, because of the shortage of lifeboats

News of the disaster did not only attract many claimed predictions—many of which were probably conceived after the event—it also attracted a great many claims made by people who said that they had been going to sail on the ship but something had happened to make them change their minds at the last minute. In fact the number of people claiming this apparently amounts to twice the capacity of the actual ship.

Sowden

Of the many supposed predictions relating to the *Titanic* some are obviously more convincing than others. One of the most disturbing is the claim made by Captain W. Sowden of the Salvation Army that he felt that a dying girl had had a vision about the *Titanic* disaster. The girl was called Jessie, the date was 14 April and the time was around three and a half hours before the *Titanic*'s collision with the iceberg.

Just before she died Jessie seemed to become delirious and spoke to Captain Sowden of being able to see a big ship sinking and many people drowning. Obviously this was nonspecific, but she then went on to mention that someone called Wally was playing the fiddle and was coming to Captain Sowden.

This did not seem to make much sense to Captain Sowden at the time, but when the facts of the sinking of the *Titanic* became known it was found that the band had played on the ship throughout the disaster to try to be a comfort to the passengers. The name of the bandmaster was Wally Hartley and he and all the rest of the band died in the disaster.

Wally was the name of the person that Jessie saw playing the fiddle in her vision. She had spoken of Wally coming to Captain Sowden and in fact the captain had known Wally Hartley some years before but had lost track of him. He certainly had not known that he was on the *Titanic*.

Sadly, Jessie died after she told Captain Sowden of her vision. However, Captain Sowden was adamant about what she had said and stated that the girl's vision had changed his spiritual outlook. In any case it is difficult to be totally sceptical about this report if Captain Sowden got it right because of the presence of Wally.

Blanche Marshall

Another reported claim of premonition of disaster relating to the *Titanic*, described in *The Paranormal—A Modern Perspective* by John Spencer, also carries elements that are difficult to ignore. A woman called Blanche Marshall is said to have gone with her husband to join the crowd that had gathered to watch the *Titanic* sail past the Isle of Wight. She is said to have called out to her husband that the ship was going to sink before it reached its destination in America and that he should do something to prevent it going any further. She also spoke of seeing many people struggling for life in icy water. All her husband did was to feel embarrassed and angry that she was making an exhibition of herself.

Unlike Jessie's account, Blanche's prediction made no mention of a specific person. It is, however, on other counts amazingly specific.

Lusitania
Furthermore, Blanche Marshall went on to give other evidence of strange predictory powers. Some years later the Marshalls booked a voyage on the *Lusitania* to America, but Blanche Marshall insisted on changing the booking because the ship was going to sink on that voyage at the hands of the Germans, with whom the British were then at war. She was clearly quite specific about her prediction because she had been happy to sail on the *Lusitania* on an earlier voyage.

Her prediction unfortunately turned out to be accurate. The *Lusitania* was sunk off the Irish coast by a German submarine on 7 May 1915.

It is very difficult to write off either of Blanche Marshall's predictions as coincidence. Both were too specific for that. It is even more difficult to write off the two predictions taken together. Blanche's predictions do seem to point to some strange power of the mind to see things in the future, incredible though this may seem.

Harris
There were other claimed predictions relating to the *Titanic* disaster, which also have something of a ring of truth about them. One of the passengers due to sail on the doomed liner was H. B. Harris, a theatre impresario.

When a wire was received by his family telling of his decision to return home on the liner, one of his friends, William Klein, had a premonition of disaster and wired back to beg Harris not to sail on the *Titanic*. Harris wired back to say that he was sticking to his original plan, whereupon Klein asked another of Harris's friends to help him try to dissuade Harris from returning home on the *Titanic*. Whatever anyone said, however, Harris seemed determined to ignore Klein's worries and duly sailed on the *Titanic*. He was one of the many who perished when the ship sank.

Although Klein's concern was based on a fairly non-specific premonition in that he did not specify why Harris should not proceed with his plans, it was real enough for him to commit himself to contacting Harris and trying to enlist the help of friends in trying to dissuade him from sailing. Presumably the wires represented concrete proof and presumably they were seen by people other than the sender and the recipient.

Futility

An interesting aspect of prediction relating to the sinking of the *Titanic* is that there were various works of fiction written before the disaster that bore strange resemblances to some aspects of the sinking of the ship. Probably the most famous of these was a novel entitled *Futility*, written by Morgan Robertson in 1898.

The ship in *Futility* was called the *Titan*. Like the *Titanic* it was what would now be known as state-of-the-art, was regarded as being unsinkable and had too few lifeboats for the size of the vessel. The size, passenger capacity and design similarities between the two ships were very striking. Both ships sailed in the month of April and both hit icebergs.

There were other similarities between the two vessels and there were differences too, although the latter are not usually dwelt upon. Perhaps the remarkable similarities can be put down to coincidence but it could suggest some ESP power of the author's mind.

The sinking of the *Titanic* struck horror into the hearts of most people and it became very well known. Probably because it was such a mega-disaster it attracted an unusual number of claimed predictions, some of which were very probably the result of fraud or hoax and some of which might have been able to be put down to sheer coincidence. Others might have been a result of people 'prophesying' after the event. Nevertheless it would appear that in some claimed predictions at least there might have been at least an element of the paranormal.

The importance of the incidence of prediction with regard to the *Titanic* is shown in the fact that a whole book has been devoted to exploring the subject. George Behe published a work entitled *Titanic—Psychic Forewarnings of a Tragedy* in which he catalogues and reports on a number of these.

Flixborough
On 2 June 1974 in the late afternoon, around 4.30 p.m., a

huge explosion took place at a chemical plant on Humberside. The explosion was indeed massive and damaged a vast number of buildings, destroying practically the whole complex around the plant. More importantly, twenty eight people were killed and hundreds injured in the explosion.

Again there is an example here of a claimed prediction occurring in connection with a disaster. Earlier the same day, around midday, a young woman was watching television in Cleethorpes, some twenty miles or so from Flixborough, when she claimed to see a newsflash in which news was given of an explosion at Flixborough that had claimed several lives.

She mentioned the fact to a couple who were in the house with her before the explosion took place. Thus there were witnesses to the claimed prediction. Furthermore it was a very specific prediction, not just a vague warning of some unnamed disaster.

Flight 401

Towards midnight on 9 December 1972 an American L–1011 of flight number 401 crashed in the Florida Everglades. Plane crashes are tragic but they are relatively common. However, there was something strange about this one.

It had been reported two weeks before the crash by an air stewardess with Eastern Airlines (the airline to which the crashed plane belonged) that she had had a vision of an L–1011 crashing at night over the Florida

Everglades. She claimed to have 'seen' the left wing and fuselage crash to the ground and to have heard people screaming.

The stewardess, whose name was not released to protect her privacy, had told her fellow crew about the vision and predicted that a crash like this would happen very near New Year. She also told her colleagues that they and she would not be involved in the crash but would have some kind of narrow escape.

In fact on the night of the actual crash the stewardess was scheduled to be part of the crew on the plane that crashed but there was a last-minute change of personnel and she did not fly in it. It would seem that she had had a very narrow escape indeed.

This was such a specific prediction and such a well-documented one that it is difficult not to see some evidence of ESP or some other force at work. To regard it as coincidence seems to be to try to stretch coincidence too far. Yet there seems to have been no suggestion of a hoax.

Goddard

Claimed examples of precognition are not by any means precise pictures of what is going to happen in the future. There can be some degree of variation and yet the precognition can still be very striking and still generally close to what does happen.

Sometimes it is the predicted ending that varies. This was true of the case involving Air Marshal Sir Victor

Goddard of the Royal New Zealand Air Force and Gerald Gladstone, a Royal Navy Officer who was later to become Admiral Sir Gerald Gladstone.

When Goddard was the guest of the British consul, General G. A. Ogden, at a party in Shanghai in January 1946, the night before he was due to fly home, he overheard Gladstone talking about him in relation to a crash, not realizing that Goddard was present. It transpired that Gladstone had had a sudden, very clear vision of seeing Goddard in a DC–3 plane that ran into a snowstorm and crashed on to a shingle beach after flying over a mountain. Goddard and the other people in the plane, including three civilians—two Englishmen and a girl—were all killed.

Clearly this was not a pleasant piece of news to receive as one is about to go on a journey but Goddard, although he was due to fly to Tokyo in a DC–3 the next morning on his way home to New Zealand, was not unduly worried. This was not because he had no belief in psychic powers but because his circumstances did not equate with those described by Gladstone. He was to be accompanied only by two of his staff officers and no civilians.

By the end of the evening, however, his circumstances had changed. Various people, including Ogden and a female secretary who had to attend an urgent meeting in Tokyo as soon as possible, and a London newspaper reporter, were all given seats on the plane.

The DC–3 took off next morning and ran into snow in the afternoon. The plane was off course, and they found themselves unexpectedly flying over mountains. The radio had failed and the plane was very low on fuel so the pilot looked for somewhere to land in what was now a bad snowstorm. Below was a small village with a strip of shingly beach.

As the plane tried to land there Goddard could not help thinking of Gladstone's vision. After some unsuccessful attempts to land the pilot at last succeeded but the plane's undercarriage collapsed and the plane spun across the shingle to come to a halt facing the sea. You can imagine what Goddard's thoughts were during the landing procedure.

In the light of the fact that Gladstone's vision had been right up to the very end Goddard was amazed to find that he and the other occupants of the plane were all still alive. He was able to testify to the accuracy of the rest of Gladstone's vision. I am sure that he was extremely glad that Gladstone had not got it quite right.

Godley

Another well-known case in the history of precognition also demonstrates the potentially imperfect nature of foreknowledge of the future. Reported by Reuben Stone in *Mysteries of the Mind*, for once it is not a tale of death and disaster.

When studying at Oxford in March 1946 the Hon. John Raymond Godley had a dream one night in which he himself appeared reading the next day's evening newspaper. He was reading the racing results and noted two horses that had won their races at odds of 7–1. One horse was called Brindal and the other was called Juladin.

He and a friend both consulted the papers the next day and found that horses of that name were indeed running that day on different race courses. Brindal was running first and Godley put money on it. When it won he put his winnings on Juladin, which also won.

So far so good. The precognition had been spot-on. However, there were imperfections in that the odds quoted in the dream were a little on the optimistic side. The starting price of Brindal was 5–4 and the starting price of Juladin was 5–2. Still it is an impressive account of precognition for all that.

There was some corroboration of his account of precognition in that he told some friends before the races. In fact some of them shared in his good fortune since they too bet on the horses.

Inaccuracies

The names of the horses that Godley dreamt about, or at least the names that he remembered in the morning after dreaming, were not always absolutely accurate. For example, he once woke up remembering the name Tubermore but could not identify a horse of that name. However, he backed one called Tuberose that was running in the Grand National that day and it won. Perhaps his supposed gift of precognition got it slightly wrong but it is perhaps just as likely that he misremembered the name.

Godley's story also points to another aspect of precognition. Like telepathy, it is not something that you can switch on to order. Far from it. The dreams about likely winners were erratic, although they were still more regular than most examples of precognition. Some people have only one predictory dream, vision or premonition in a lifetime—and most people have none, or at least no major, memorable ones. Also the dreams stopped as suddenly as they had begun, after a particularly advantageous bet.

Nostradamus

One of the figures most commonly associated with predictions is Nostradamus. He was a French physician and clairvoyant who lived in the sixteenth century (1503–1566) and whose predictions are still thought to be relevant today.

He is said by some to have been responsible for a wide range of important predictions, some of them referring to quite recent times. These include the foreseeing of the Napoleonic Wars, the French Revolution, the American Civil War, the abdication of Edward VIII, the rise and fall of Adolf Hitler, and the assassination of President Kennedy. If even some of this is true then he clearly had quite a gift.

There is, however, a major problem with the writings of Nostradamus. They are very difficult to interpret. Supposedly to avoid the attention of the Inquisition, he wrote in quatrains in a pastiche of languages. His writing was a mixture of Greek, Latin, French and local dialect. As if this were not enough, he included in the text obscure expressions that later interpreters took to be anagrams.

Some of the difficulties involved in interpreting his meaning can be put down to the changing of details of the kind that sometimes occur in predictions. This has been mentioned above in some of the other claimed cases of precognition, such as the horse called Tuberose that seemed to appear in Godley's dream as Tubermore. It is for this reason that 'Hister' is thought to be a corruption of 'Hitler'.

Because of the difficulty in interpreting the obscure quatrains of Nostradamus people have been unable to say whether his writings are predictions, or of what they are predictions, until an event that seems to fit one of these. Even then some straining of the imagination and of the intellect is necessary to make some of the details fit. The whole thing is a matter of interpreting his words in the light of hindsight.

The Rill letters

The Rill letters were much clearer in their precognition than the quatrains of Nostradamus. They were written by Andreas Rill in 1914, when he was serving in the German army near Colmar in Alsace, to his family in Bavaria. The letters, two in number, concerned the predictions made by a French prisoner while Rill and other soldiers were questioning him.

It is not clear exactly who the Frenchman was, although he appears to have been a civilian rather than a member of the French army. Rill described him as a 'holy man', and Rill was billeted in a Capuchin monastery in Sigolsheim, near Colmar. There was a suggestion that he was once a rich man who had given away his wealth and joined the monastery.

Some of the Frenchman's predictions reported by Rill were quite extraordinary. For example, he predicted that the war in which Rill was a soldier would last five years and that Germany would lose it. The war was World War I and the year was 1914.

In fact World War I lasted four years and three months, but this is the kind of discrepancy that is found in other examples of precognition. The important thing to remember is that at the time Rill was questioning the Frenchman the war was thought to be going to last only a short time, the general feeling being that it would 'all be over by Christmas'. Certainly, few people in August 1914 would have expected it to last anything like five years, or even four years.

Rill's reporting of the Frenchman's prediction of what was certainly Hitler showed the same slight discrepancy that shows in many other claimed examples of precognition. The Frenchman predicted that an Antichrist would be born and would become a dictator in Germany in 1932. In fact, the Nazis gained power in the elections of January 1933.

He predicted that in 1938 preparations for another war

would begin, that it would last three years, that Italy would fight with Germany and that the outcome of the war would be the downfall of the dictator. Of these predictions only the length of the war is a bit out.

If Rill reported on the Frenchman's predictions correctly, and there seems no need to assume that he did not, it would appear that the Frenchman had some strange power that transcended the power of the ordinary senses. Admittedly not all his predictions were accurate but those that proved to be right outnumbered those that proved to be wrong by quite a margin. As has been seen, there were some imprecise details among accurate predictions, but this is not unusual in cases of precognition.

The predictions of the Frenchman questioned by Rill seem so extraordinary that, of course, some form of fraud was suspected. Many sceptics were of the opinion that the letters from Rill were a forgery, put together after World War II when all the facts about it were known.

Rill's son declared that the facts intimated in the letters were practically common knowledge in the area around Untermuhlhausen where the Rills lived long before World War II. Obviously he could have been said to be prejudiced.

However, Dr Hans Bender of Germany's Freiburg Institute had the Rill letters examined by forensic scientists who found no evidence of fraud or alteration. Other things mentioned in Rill's letters with the relevant records were found to be true and genuine.

Rill himself had obviously been intrigued by the Frenchman and his predictions, long before they could be proved or disproved. By chance he was stationed near the monastery at Sigolsheim again, at Turckheim, near the end of the war in 1918. He tried to find the Frenchman again, but he was told by the people at the monastery that he had died earlier that same year.

This at least gave Bender a clue, and they searched the records of the Capuchin monasteries in Sigolsheim or the surrounding area for details of a French monk who had died in 1918. They could find none. However, they did uncover the fact that there had been a guest at the monastery in Sigolsheim who had died in 1918 before Rill arrived to try to find him.

The guest was known as Frater Laicus, but apart from that no details were forthcoming. There was speculation that Frater Laicus might have been a wealthy man who had given his money to the monastery and thus was allowed to stay there as a permanent official guest. However, Frater Laicus remains an enigma.

Ordinary people

These then are a few recorded famous cases of claimed precognition. In ordinary families, however, there are many tales of precognition, although it almost certainly will not be called that. Obviously these cases will not have been officially documented, the details will have become a little hazy in the passing on of the story, the details will probably have become more than a little exaggerated or embroidered in the telling as time has passed and the story may have been apocryphal in the first place.

The stories are frequently related to disasters. Some of these relate to major disasters that have affected a number of people. Others relate to more personal disasters or misfortunes.

Some families have handed on stories relating to the sinking of the *Titanic*. Most of these relate to a relative who was booked on the liner, or who was planning to sail on the liner, but who had a change of mind and plans after having had some form of premonition. Most of these tales will have little or no truth in them. As has been mentioned above, far more people, even at the time, claimed to have changed their minds about sailing because of a premonition than the liner could possibly have accommodated. Doubtless in the following years the number of people claiming this would have increased.

There seems to be something ghoulishly attractive about disaster, provided you are not actually involved. It seems to give some people a frisson to connect themselves with disaster.

This is why, whenever a plane crashes, there is bound to be a number of accounts circulating informally all over the place about people or their relatives, friends or neighbours, who had being going to take that flight but had had a 'feeling' about it and had decided not to go. It is difficult not to be sceptical and cynical about such a predictable response, although among all these rather spurious claims there may occasionally be a genuine one.

A great many accounts of premonitions, dreams and visions relate to domestic situations rather than to national disasters. It is quite common for people to become convinced that they had a premonition or dream about a close relative who has died or been killed. Unfortunately, they often do not mention this fact until after the death has been reported and made known to them.

For this reason it is easy to be sceptical and cynical about such accounts, and certainly a great many of them will be the results of supposed predictions that happened after the event or the result of some strange desire to play some kind of part in disaster. However, once again there may well be some genuine examples of some strange predictory power of the mind among such accounts.

It is difficult to know unless the cases have been documented. There is a problem with making sure that there are witnesses to the claimed prediction before the occurrence of the event that the premonition, dream or vision relates to. Sometimes the premonition or vision occurs very close in time to the relevant event. It may be an overnight dream that relates to an event that was taking place at the time of the dream and is reported early the next morning.

In addition people who have experienced a premonition, dream or vision that seems to predict disaster are often emotionally upset and agitated. They are too busy rushing around trying to contact relatives to find out if they are all right or to forewarn them of possible impending disaster to think of getting someone to act as witness to what they have claimed to have predicted.

For those who feel that they have had a premonition or what appears to be a predictory dream or vision there is a possibility of documenting this officially so that it can be looked at later in the light of future events relating to the claimed precognition. Premonitions can be registered with the British Premonitions Bureau.

The people who run this claim that they have some indications that there is some kind of unusual phenomenon at work. Peter Fairley, one of the people who set up the Premonitions Bureau, is on record as having pointed to a problem about trying to prove the existence of some form of predictory power. It is that when there is early evidence that someone has predictory powers and investigation into thishas begun, the power seems to disappear. It cannot be turned on like a tap. Obviously this has important implications for researchers in labs trying to investigate premonitions, visions and visionary dreams.

Another problem with predictions relating to domestic activities is that it is not known how many premonitions or dreams turn out to relate to events that did not take place. It is very common for us to have odd feelings or feelings of dread relating to someone or something that turn out to have no foundation, although quite a long time scale can be involved in prediction.

Some people of Celtic descent seem to have a greater connection with precognition than others. In the Highlands of Scotland, for example, it is not at all unusual to hear accounts of women who had, or indeed have, what is known as 'second sight' or even 'the gift'. Someone of my acquaintance claims, according to family history or legend, that her great-grandmother's friend forecast her own death by burning, and many years later she was indeed burned to death in her cottage. Similar tales abound in many Highland and Irish families.

Summary
Thus we have a picture of some of the claims made on behalf of precognition. There is much scepticism related to the supposed phenomenon, particularly among scientists. However, many ordinary people, although they may place no credence in the claimed predictions of supposed fortune-tellers, may have a sneaking feeling that there may be something in it, particularly if they know something of some of the reported cases, such as those connected with the Aberfan disaster.

Scientists meanwhile are at work trying to find out more about the supposed phenomenon. One of their areas of research has been into dreams.

Dreams and REM sleep
There is a problem with trying to monitor dreams because, although we are all said to dream, we usually either forget that we have had dreams at all or forget

the content of them as soon as we wake up. There has been scientific research into sleep and dreams that shows that the most vivid and striking dreams take place during what is known as rapid eye movement sleep, also known as paradoxical sleep.

During rapid eye movement (REM) sleep the eyes dart rapidly back and forth although the eyelids remained closed. Scientists, by monitoring people who are asleep, have observed that such rapid eye activity occurs at regular intervals throughout the night.

Of great importance to anyone interested in dream precognition, and indeed in dreams generally, is the fact that research indicates that if a person is woken at the end of a period of rapid eye movement he or she is much more likely to report a dream than if he or she is asked on wakening normally if any dreaming has occurred and any details of them remembered. If sleepers are woken after a period of ordinary sleep when rapid eye movement is not taking place they are much less likely to report a dream, except that if people are woken during the first hour of sleep before the first period of rapid eye movement they often report dreams.

This could one day have important implications for the suggested phenomenon of precognitive dreaming but of course such research of this kind into the paranormal is costly. It is also likely to be very slow because of the difficulty of identifying suitable subjects and because of the fact that, although a supposedly suitable subject may have many dreams, very few of these dreams are likely to be precognitive. As has been pointed out earlier in the chapter it is of the essence of supposed precognition that it cannot be switched on at will. Indeed the precognitive ability seems to desert people if they are subjected to laboratory conditions. Cynics will make the most of this.

Future

While some people are trying to get more information about precognition through dreams others are speculating about the nature of time and the nature of the future. They suggest that more than one future might be a possibility and that time might be constantly breaking up into different 'timelines'.

This is as yet beyond the understanding of most of us. Indeed someone predicting the future may seem more credible to us.

Summary

Although our intellects may deny the fact that it is possible to predict the future, the intuition of many of us, and even our experience of life, may tell us otherwise.

For the moment all we can really be sure of is the fact that there have been a number of predictions that have been attested to by witnesses and fully documented with no proven sign of fraud or hoax. Until science proves or disproves otherwise we may just have to accept, however reluctantly, that the mind in certain individuals can be a predictive force.

Chapter 4

Clairvoyance

'Clairvoyance' is derived form the French words *clair*, 'clear' and *voir*, 'to see'. It does not, however, mean clear-sightedness or clear sight. In fact it is a branch of what is known as ESP or extrasensory perception and has associations both with telepathy and precognition, being the ability to detect or acquire information by some perception other than those of the five senses.

Indeed people often refer to someone who claims to be able to draw on some psychic powers to predict someone's future as a clairvoyant. Thus if they went to consult someone who claimed to be able to tell someone's future by means of a crystal ball they might well talk of going to consult a clairvoyant. Likewise, if someone wished to have a tarot card-reading carried out, he or she might well speak of going to see a clairvoyant.

Clairvoyance is also sometimes used to refer to precognition, to the ability to see things that are going to happen in the future. For example, Nostradamus, who made so many strangely worded predictions, many of which have been declared by hindsight by many to be accurate, has been described as a clairvoyant.

The future and predictions are not, however, a necessary part of clairvoyance. As has been mentioned above, clairvoyance is the ability to detect and acquire information about objects—and people—and events by ESP. In this respect it is allied to telepathy although, unlike telepathy, the transference of information in clairvoyance need not be on a person-to-person basis.

People consult clairvoyants for many reasons relating to their claimed ability to see things and happenings that others cannot be aware of, using their normal senses. Clairvoyants are sought out by people wishing to find something or someone or to find out what actually happened in relation to a particular incident.

Missing persons
One of the areas of modern life in which clairvoyants are sometimes involved is that of missing persons. They are frequently consulted by relatives who have often failed to find information by any other means and who have become desperate.

It is one of the sad facts of life today that many people go missing without leaving any kind of message to account for their decision and without giving any indication as to their whereabouts. Very often they are young people but older people, often husbands and wives, also disappear.

This leaves relatives in a terrible situation. They have no way of knowing what has happened to the person. They may have had no inkling that anything was wrong or at least that things had got to such an extreme state.

Naturally, in a good many cases they fear that the person who has gone has been in an accident and they frenziedly ring the police and hospitals. When they draw a blank at the hospitals they start worrying in case the missing person has been murdered or abducted.

It must be a terrible feeling to be in such a situation. Even the police are not in a position to be all that helpful unless the person is under age or there is some evidence of foul play. There is nothing in the law to prevent adults from walking out if they please.

People's reasons for going missing are various. They tend to vary according to age. Young people often leave because they have no jobs and no prospects and they think these will be more plentiful in a big city, such as London. There was a time when this was true but it is no longer quite so true, and many young people arrive there only to find that they remain jobless and penniless and have to sleep rough.

Often they are too proud to ring home or contact their parents by letter. They just disappear and their parents worry themselves into a state of desperation because they simply do not know what has happened. The parents' thoughts may well still be on murder and abduction.

There is often a sadder or more sinister reason. Young people frequently leave home because they do not get on with their parents or step-parents. Sometimes the reason is that they have been abused, even sexually abused, by a parent or step-parent.

In the case of adults the situation is sometimes more

complex. Some leave because they are involved in another relationship in another place and cannot pluck up courage to admit to it. Others leave because they cannot cope, either at home or at work, and are at the end of their tether. Sadly, some leave because they have been declared redundant and are too ashamed to admit it to others.

The point of all this seeming irrelevance is that the relatives who are left following the departure of a missing person are left in a state of limbo with little or no information to go on. They can hire a private detective but this can be expensive and often seems to have little chance of success. There are agencies such as the Salvation Army that try to help and there are helplines by which a missing person can get a message to a relative without his or her whereabouts being revealed.

Faced with this bleak picture in which they do not know where the missing person is or whether he or she is still alive and well, relatives will try anything that might give them at least a clue. It is in this state of mind that several of them seek the help of a clairvoyant, although some may have enough faith in ESP to do so early on in their search for the missing person.

But what can the clairvoyant do? Those who describe themselves as clairvoyants and those who believe in their powers claim that they may be able to give a clue to where the missing person might be, if they cannot actually locate them.

In fact I know someone personally who claims to have

been helped in this way. The clairvoyant may have helped but, on the other hand, the place where the relative, a young daughter in this case, was located seemed fairly predictable.

Perhaps this is unfair. It cannot have seemed that predictable to the parents or they would have thought of it right away without help. If people find solace in consulting a clairvoyant it may well be a good thing as long as false hopes are not raised.

There are other situations in which people seek the advice of clairvoyants to try to take advantage of their supposed ability to locate people and objects. One of these concerns attempts by adopted children to find their birth parents.

Because of a change in legislation it is now much easier to locate at least birth mothers than it used to be. In addition, there are agencies that offer help and counselling. However, there are cases in which adoptees simply draw a blank and it is then that they sometimes turn to clairvoyants.

People in general tend to be cynical about clairvoyance as they tend to be about most things involving ESP or the paranormal. Certainly, some degree of success is claimed on behalf of clairvoyants but some people claim that they get quite a lot of their information from their clients themselves by skilful questioning, without the clients being aware of this and sometimes without the clients even being aware that they were in possession of the information.

However, in the case of the location of dead bodies of missing persons it is difficult to see how this latter objection can be relevant. Certainly there are in existence reports of people who have helped to locate dead bodies by giving information that they seem not to have been able to get hold of by normal means.

If in fact there is such a thing as clairvoyance it could be of enormous value to the police in finding missing persons, dead or alive, and in detecting crimes. Many people feel that there is much more evidence of clairvoyance around than is ever reported.

They feel that either people keep such thoughts to themselves—being probably extremely surprised, and perhaps upset, at having had seemingly clairvoyant thoughts—or else that they may tell a few close friends who may sympathize but who scoff or just forget all about it. They might think of telling a friendly neighbourhood police officer, but they will probably decide against that in case, however politely, they are made to look ever so slightly mad. Perhaps if clairvoyance, precognition and ESP generally were given a better press we would hear of more successful examples of it.

Mme Vuagniaux

One case in which clairvoyant help seems to have been instrumental in finding a missing person, or rather the dead body of a missing person, took place in 1904. The case concerns Dr Harold Munch Petersen from Copenhagen.

He was on a kind of mini-tour of Europe and wrote to his sister that he was on his way to Aix-les-Bains. She heard no more from him and never saw him again.

The doctor should have gone to Paris from Aix, but the French police could find no trace of him in Paris or find any evidence that he had ever arrived there. It was established that he had arrived in Aix and had said that he was going to climb Mont du Chat, one of the most dangerous mountains in the neighbourhood of Aix. A search was made on this and other mountains in the area but nothing was found.

An anonymous letter was sent to a local magistrate claiming knowledge of the fact that the doctor had been killed on a precipice on the Revard, near a spot where there was an old house sometimes used as a shelter for sheep in bad weather. Searches were made on the basis of the information but nothing was found.

The magistrate, by means of a little detection, discovered that the letter had been written by Mme Vuagniaux, the wife of a local artist. On being contacted, she gave more details to the police but again nothing was found. Just as Mme Vuagniaux and her husband were planning to go and look for the doctor's body themselves, a farmer found the body in an area that he hardly ever went to. It lay at the foot of a precipice.

The spot was a remote one that was rarely visited by anyone and had never been visited by Mme Vuagniaux. Many of the details that she had given about the nature of the location of the body turned out to be accurate. Yet it is difficult to know how she could possibly have got these details using only the normal senses.

Croiset
A Dutchman who claimed to have clairvoyant powers is said to have been instrumental in locating the body of a boy who had drowned. Since he was also instrumental in detecting a murder, details of his supposed successes are given below under 'Crime detection'.

Crime detection
There may be a good deal of ambivalence around about the attitude to clairvoyants but there is one area in which some of them seem to have achieved some success. This is in the area of crime detection.

Hurkos
Perhaps the best known clairvoyant who was involved in crime detection was a Dutch house painter named Peter Hurkos. His psychic powers seem to have had their roots in an accident that he sustained. In 1943 he fell from a ladder to the ground thirty-five feet below and suffered a fractured skull. He was taken to the Zuidwal hospital in the Hague.

He was in a coma, and when he regained consciousness he is said to have displayed unusual powers. He is said to have warned a fellow patient who was being discharged not to leave because something terrible would happen to him. He even tried to engage the doctor's help in stopping the man but the man left.Hurkos claimed to know that the man was a British agent, although he could not have acquired this information by any normal means.

He also claimed that something terrible was going to happen to the man, that he was going to be killed by the Gestapo in Kalverstaat in a few days' time. Two days later the man was killed by the Gestapo in Kalverstaat.

As well as predicting that something terrible would happen to the British agent, Hurkos is said to have astonished his fellow patients by telling them things about themselves that he could not have known. Of course sceptics will say that he could have found out at least some of this from remarks made by the patients or from questioning the patients subtly and skilfully without them realizing it.

He went on to show unusual powers when he left hospital and was involved in trying to locate missing persons using his supposed clairvoyant powers. It is said that he helped the police of Scotland Yard in their search for the Stone of Destiny.

This was a stone, originally located in Scone in Scotland, an ancient seat of the kings of Scotland and connected with the throning of kings. It had been removed to England by Edward I to become part of coronation ceremonies in Westminster Abbey but in 1950 was stolen by Scottish nationalists. The stone was retrieved, although some claim that it was not the original that was sent back to London.

Afterwards Hurkos became involved in some American crimes. He is said to have been instrumental in 1958 in helping the Miami police in the investigaton of two crimes, one the murder of a taxi-driver. By sitting in the taxi of the murdered man, Hurkos was able to give the police a fairly detailed description of the man whom they were seeking.

He was then called in to help the police in Boston who were trying to identify the Boston Strangler, a man who in the early 1960s was sexually assaulting and murdering women in their own homes. Even those members of the police who were at first inclined to be extremely cynical about the chances of Hurkos being of any significant help were said to have been very surprised at some of the information with which he was able to supply them.

Hurkos would use various objects associated with the crime and photographs of scenes of the crime or of objects connected with the crimes to get information. For example, he would examine articles of clothing that had been removed from the scene of the crime by the police.

In the course of doing so he is said to have astonished the police by being able to describe some of the murders so closely that he might have been present at the time, which he obviously was not. His information impressed the police partly because it contained elements relating to the murders that they already knew but details of which had not been revealed to the public. It would appear that there was no way in which Hurkos could have known about this information by normal means.

Hurkos came up with a detailed description of the

Boston Strangler and identified someone whom he considered to be the murderer although the police were more interested in someone else. In the end a man called Albert DeSalvo confessed to the crime. Since he was in possession of information relating to the crimes and the scenes of crimes the police accepted his confession.

Many of the details that Hurkos gave the police about the likely murderer also fitted DeSalvo, but apparently Hurkos still held that his suspect was the real murderer. In any event, DeSalvo did not go to trial because the confession was made to a psychiatrist and under Massachusetts law a doctor who receives information from a patient cannot use it as evidence.

DeSalvo was sent to prison for other crimes of which he was convicted. He was found stabbed to death in his cell in Walpole Prison in Massachusetts in 1973.

Hurkos might not have agreed with the police about the identity of the murderer but there seems no doubt that he was extremely useful to the police in their search. He certainly enabled them to narrow the field of their search, and he impressed greatly many of those who saw him in action.

The Dutch clairvoyant was also called in to help with what was known as the Hollywood Massacre, in which Sharon Tate, second wife of Roman Polanski, the Polish film director, was murdered. Hurkos was called in not by the police but by a lawyer who was a friend of another victim, Jay Sebring.

The Los Angeles police were said to have been quite

impressed by Hurkos who examined the house where the murders had taken place, studying objects there and the bloodstains. Much of what he told the police about the murders is said to have been accurate but he did not indicate to them that a woman was involved in the murders, as turned out to be the case. It was not only Charles Manson who was involved but other members of his group or cult.

Since Hurkos was not called in officially by the police, his role in the case of the Hollywood Massacre was not as well documented as his role in the case of the Boston Strangler. However, in both cases he seems to have demonstrated the ability to gather information and draw conclusions by means other than those of the normal five senses.

Croiset

One of Hurkos's fellow countrymen, Gerald Croiset, also seems to have demonstrated extraordinary powers. He is said to have made many claims of information acquired by paranormal means. Much of this is said to have been too nonspecific to make a decision about and much is said to have been inaccurate.

However, there are at least two cases in which he is reported to have been helpful, both of these involving children. The children were both declared missing and were both found to be dead.

One of these was a boy who had been missing for twelve days when Croiset was called in, the police having thus far failed to find the boy—dead or alive. Obviously the boy's parents were frantic.

The supposedly clairvoyant Croiset said immediately that the boy was dead, sent the police a sketch of the area where the boy had met his death and described a weather vane that was connected with the area. He went to the Hague and identified a place that answered his description of the place where the boy had died.

Although they had not mentioned the fact to Croiset the police had already been led to that spot by their tracker dogs. They had found nothing.

Croiset said that the boy had drowned in the river at that spot. He predicted that the boy's body would surface about half a mile from the spot where he had drowned in four days' time. The body surfaced as Croiset had predicted. There was another strange thing connected with the event. After Croiset told the police what he thought had happened, the police had dragged the river at the spot where Croiset claimed the boy had drowned and at the spot where he predicted the body would surface. They found nothing.

Like Hurkos, in some cases Croiset seems to have demonstrated a strange ability to have information about the whereabouts of objects or people and the ability to know details about events that have occurred as well as powers of precognition. The seeming clairvoyant powers of Hurkos were demonstrated in another case involving a child.

His help was sought in helping to find information

about a little girl who had gone missing. Croiset is supposed right away to have told the person who contacted him by telephone that the girl was dead and to have described the building where her body was.

He gave an early description of the murderer and gave more details when he had examined some of the little girl's clothing and had looked at some of the photographs relating to the case. His description was quite close to that of the person who was found to be the murderer, although there were some inaccuracies in it.

The Yorkshire Ripper

There are certain situations that attract a whole series of offers of supposedly clairvoyant help. One of these is an event involving a missing child. Another is mass murder or serial killing.

An example of serial killing that attracted a great many offers of help from supposed clairvoyants was that perpetrated by the murderer in the north of England who became known as the Yorkshire Ripper. The killings began in 1975, and over a period of about five years thirteen women were killed, several of them being prostitutes. They were all killed in a similar way and were badly mutilated, a screwdriver being used to make multiple stab wounds.

Many people claiming psychic powers contacted police or the media with supposed descriptions of the murderer. Most of these were demonstrated to be nothing like the description of the man who was finally convicted of the murders. However, some information given to the *Yorkshire Post* by a woman did prove to contain some surprisingly accurate details.

In fact the account of these was not published in the paper because of the guidelines laid down by the police about publicity relating to the case. The woman, named Nellie Jones, predicted that a killing would take place on 17 November or 27 November of that year and there was a killing on 17 November.

She also gave some details of the murderer. She said that he was a lorry driver who drove a lorry with a name on the cab beginning with the letter 'C', that his name was Peter and that he lived in Bradford in a house with the number 6, which had wrought iron gates and steps up to the door.

The man who was later convicted of the murders was indeed called Peter, Peter Sutcliffe. He was a lorry driver for a firm called Clark Transport and lived at 6 Garden Lane in Bradford with gates and steps as Nellie Jones had described.

Obviously there are resemblances between the details related by Nellie Jones and the details relating to the murderer, Peter Sutcliffe. Perhaps these details would have been useful if they had been made known, although, as is the case in accounts of precognition, it is common for there to be inaccuracies as well as accuracies in accounts. On the other hand there was such a plethora of accounts that were not at all accurate that it is difficult to separate the sheep from the goats, to know what is likely to be helpful and what is likely to be garbage.

Travelling clairvoyance

This is a phenomenon that refers to a claim that someone has been able to 'visit' psychically another place at some distance. It is different from an out-of-body experience in that it is not claimed that the body is left physically behind. This is also known as 'remote viewing' and is described in Chapter 5, Out-of-Body Experiences.

Summary

If you consider some of the above examples of supposed clairvoyance it is difficult to see how all the details could have been ascertained using the usual five senses, unless there was some form of fraud or hoax going on, which in these cases seems unlikely. Coincidence is always a possibility but too many claims can be made on behalf of coincidence. It can be stretched too far.

Why are there so few convincing recorded cases of successful clairvoyance? This may have more to say about the lack of documentation than the lack of clairvoyance. Perhaps if that could be improved then we would also see an increased incidence of successful clairvoyance.

It has been mentioned above that people who claim to have had some form of clairvoyant experience are often curiously private about it. They seem to keep it to themselves or tell only a few close friends, perhaps because of fear of being met with disbelief, scorn or a kindly concern for their sanity.

The other point is that, although there are people who claim to be generally clairvoyant, it is very likely the case, as is the case with experiences of precognition, that someone may have only a very few claimed clairvoyant experiences in a lifetime—or even only one.

The ability to locate objects and people through a sense other than our usual ones and the ability to know more about events that have occurred would be of immense help to all of us, particularly to the police. Indeed, if they could couple such an ability with modern detecting procedures, such as DNA (or genetic) fingerprinting, then considerably more serious crimes might be solved.

If clairvoyants do have a strange ability to detect and acquire information of which the rest of us are ignorant, what is the source of that ability? For the moment the answer is not known. It may never be known. For the moment all we know is that it appears that a few people, and maybe more than we think, have a power of the mind that we cannot quite comprehend.

Chapter 5

Out-of-Body Experiences

So many reports circulate about what are known as out-of-body experiences that it is difficult to believe that there is nothing in any of them, that anyone who claims to have had experience of one of these has made it up. An out-of-body experience is one in which there seems to be a separation of the physical body and the intangible part of one.

This intangible part has variously been called the mind, the consciousness or the soul. People who are interested in psychic matters often refer to it as an astral body. Whatever you decide to call it, it represents our inner self, not our outer self, as the physical body does.

People who claim that they have had out-of-body experiences speak of suddenly feeling themselves rising into the air. They then speak of looking down at themselves and at the rest of the scene below. Often the people are asleep or anaesthetized when out-of-body experiences occur but this is by no means always the case.

Some claim to feel an odd sensation in their limbs before the experience occurs and some claim to feel a great pressure round their heads. Some feel as though they float up right away after this and some claim that they go through a dark tunnel first.

It is remarkable the amount of detail that some people remember after their claimed out-of-body experiences. Some of them have commented on noticing things that were on the top of their wardrobes that they had forgotten were there—a useful way of finding things that have been mislaid. Other people speak of seeming to notice for the first time the details of a pattern on a bedspread or carpet, or of how untidy a pile of shoes in the corner looks.

Audrey Bourne, whose experience is described later under 'Pain and out-of-body experiences' (*see* page 121), claims that while she was out of her body she was able to see a bald spot on the top of her head that she had not known was there. When she was back in her body and back at home she looked in the mirror and saw that she did indeed have a bald spot.

Out-of-body experiences, unlike some situations where the mind seems to be in control, are not uncommon. In *Explaining the Unexplained* (1993) by Hans J. Eysenck and Carl Sargent, the authors claim that surveys suggest that some 10 to 20 per cent of the general population claim to have had an out-of-body experience at some point in their lives. There appears to be some dispute about actual numbers and percentages, since Reuben Stone in *Mysteries of the Mind* (1993) refers to the fact that one person in four claims to have had at least one out-of-body experience in the course of his or her life.

Whatever the actual numbers are, it seems that a sig-

nificant number of us have laid claim to an out-of-body
experience. Furthermore some people claim to have experienced them repeatedly.

Near-death experiences

Many out-of-body experiences can be categorized also
as near-death experiences, sometimes abbreviated to
NDEs. Here the mind, soul or astral body seems to leave
the physical body, in times of great danger to life or even
at a time when the person involved has 'died' for a short
time and has recovered.

The fact that there seems to have been an increase in
near-death experiences or the fact that there has been an
increase in the number of us who know someone who
claims to have experienced such a phenomenon could be
put down to modern resuscitation techniques. Some of
these are a result of the new technology in medicine and
some are the result of a new awareness of what can be
done to keep people alive, a kind of extension of first
aid.

Not so long ago it was the case that if you died, you
were dead and that was it. Then resuscitation techniques
began to be used on people who seemed to have
drowned in that they seemed to be dead when they were
pulled from the water.

Such resuscitation techniques involve what is known
as mouth-to-mouth resuscitation, a procedure in which
the rescuer breathes into the mouth of the person who
seems to be unconscious or dead from drowning in an

attempt to get his or her own respiratory system going again. At the same time the patient's chest has regular pressure exerted on it to try to get it started again.

A similar technique is carried out on people who have suffered from heart attacks. If the people undertaking the resuscitation can get the treatment going in time and can keep it going until the patient comes round, until the paramedics arrive with their modern life-saving machines and procedures then the patients are often okay as long as they have not been 'out' too long and suffered brain damage.

Heart disease is rife in modern life, partly as a result of our frenzied lifestyle and unhealthy diet. Fortunately, although many more people suffer heart attacks, a greater proportion of them survive, thanks to resuscitation techniques, and a new awareness of them, and thanks to modern medical techniques and surgical procedures, such as bypass surgery and heart transplants.

I stress heart attacks because the people whom I know personally who claim to have had supposed near-death experiences have had the experience as part of a heart attack or heart surgery. In fact, I know at least three, suggesting that the experience is quite common or else that I have unduly psychic friends. All three were middle-aged men, and this is in line with heart disease statistics generally.

There is a striking similarity in different people's accounts of near-death experiences. Not all the accounts have all the aspects but many of them have.

Many of those who claim to have had near-death experiences speak of how difficult it is to describe the experience exactly. They speak of suddenly finding themselves above their bodies, looking down at themselves either as they lie on the operating theatre, on a hospital bed, or as they lie 'dead' during or just after resuscitation. The sensation that they experience when they feel that they can be something separate from their own bodies is often commented upon with surprise or even disbelief.

They often say that they felt that, although they were obviously unconscious at the time, they were still remarkably aware of what was going on around them at some points in their near-death experiences. Some speak of the people that were standing around at the time they were being resuscitated. Others speak of hearing the doctors talking in the operating theatre

In many accounts of near-death experiences people speak of travelling down a long, dark tunnel, usually rapidly, after their bodies have been left behind. A sense of great calmness and peace is central to many of the accounts. Strange sounds or noises of a ringing, buzzing or whistling nature, by no means always pleasant are often reported.

At the end of the tunnel many people report seeing family members or friends, or even people whom they knew just vaguely, who are already dead. Such people often, but not always, appear in an ordinary human form rather than in the form of what we think of as spirits.

Some feel that these people who greet them at the end of the tunnel do so to lead them on to somewhere else.

Sometimes, however, people speak not of a relative or friend guiding them but of some kind of kindly being who is suffused with light. This being may also be trying to lead them somewhere or may be showing flashbacks from the past lives of the people concerned. There is often mention of a great deal of light and whiteness around.

There is often a report of some kind of barrier, this being the barrier between life and death. The implication is that if the person in the middle of the near death experience goes over the barrier he or she will be lost to life and this world, and may possibly move on to another world. If he or she turns back from the barrier then life as it was known remains and they return to their former lives.

In several cases the being suffused with light or some other kind of agency urges the person to go back to life, or even gives the impression of giving a reprieve from death. In many such cases the person undergoing the near-death experience has someone still alive for whom he or she has a strong sense of responsibility—a child who would be left orphaned and alone if the person died, for example.

At first, or at least while they are still in the grip of the near-death experience, people speak of feeling a sense of loss or sadness when they turn back from the barrier. This lessens and often disappears when the person recovers from the near-death experience and is back to 'life' again.

Those who have gone through near-death experiences often speak of what an effect these had on the rest of their lives. Even those who were extremely afraid of death and dying seem to lose this fear and view the possibility of death with a great sense of calmness. Indeed, some speak of a general decrease in levels of anxiety and worry, as though their experiences have made them more able to cope with life and caused them to become more laid-back and more philosophical

They frequently speak of an increased concern for and sensitivity towards other people. Some even totally change their lifestyles as they feel their lives up to now have been pointless and seek what is to them a more worthwhile or purposeful lifestyle.

When they first recover from near-death experiences, or at least after they recover from the physical condition that led to the experiences, they often feel a kind of great compulsion to speak about it. This soon passes, given the incredulous or sceptical reactions that their accounts usually arise in others. Unless they wish tales of their insanity to circulate freely around the neighbourhood they tend to stop talking about their experiences fairly soon. This is rather sad, not only because it inhibits people from giving expression to how they feel but also because it tends to make the number of near-death experiences seem less than it well may be.

An American cardiologist, Michael Sabom, was originally sceptical about his patients and their near-death experiences. In his book, *Recollections of Death* (1982), he tells how he changed his mind. He found that, when he first tried to get his patients to talk to him about it, there was a marked reluctance to talk about the subject. It later emerged that this was because many of them felt that a member of the medical profession would regard accounts of near-death experiences with scepticism or think that their patients had been hallucinating.   •

When he decided to question his patients on the subject he did so in a careful, clinical way, in the same way as he would take details of medical histories. He tried to be careful not to give the patients any hint of his own scepticism.

In any case, as he went on interviewing people who had recovered from serious heart attacks or had recovered from other life-threatening situations, such as cardiac arrest during major surgery, he was forced to change his mind. He discovered that a remarkable proportion of the people who had had such life-threatening conditions, and who in some cases had temporarily 'died', gave details of what seem to have been near-death experiences.

It is extremely difficult to account for near-death experiences and to account for the scale on which they would seem to exist. Also, it is tempting to look for some kind of rational reason to account for them.

Thus, it has been suggested that near-death experiences can be attributed to anaesthetic drugs or other drugs, some of which may have hallucinatory side effects. Indeed some people have spoken of a sensation of going down a tunnel when they have been having dental anaesthesia. However, this theory hits an early problem.

It is perhaps all very well as an explanation of near-death experiences that occur during surgical operations, although many people have anaesthesia without reporting the 'tunnel' or any of the other effects described by people who undergo near-death experiences. However, several near-death experiences have been reported when people have just taken a heart attack and are perhaps in the process of being resuscitated. Thus in many cases there is no question of drugs being involved.

Suggestions have also been made that near-death experiences are simply a psychological response to physical or medical trauma, although this is rather a vague notion. An alternative theory is that the experience is the result of the depletion of the oxygen supply to the brain.

Although this depletion would seem a possibility in some cases, it should not really be a possibility in cases that occur during surgical operations since the oxygen supply is monitored carefully. Also, if the oxygen depletion was so severe as to lead to such an untoward reaction it seems unusual that the person shows no sign of mental impairment later.

It has been suggested that near-death experiences are in some way the result of the release of brain chemicals called endomorphins. Certainly the release of chemicals from the brain may be a factor in other situations in which the mind seems to be having a great deal of control of the body, such as pain control, but there is not yet evidence to show that this is the case in near-death experiences.

Another theory suggests that the near-death experience is a kind of religious wish-fulfilment, that it is a result of people who believe in Christianity wishing to make their dreams of heaven come true. There is an immediate objection to this: it is the fact that it is not just convinced Christians who seem to undergo near-death experiences—and many of these do not mention any of the aspects of heaven that are thought of as being usual, such as angels with beating wings and harps. People of other religions and, in some ways more importantly, agnostics and atheists also speak of undergoing much the same kind of experience.

Finally, it has been suggested that people who have brushes with death claim to have near-death experiences because they have heard about them from other people and know all the details. However, Dr Michael Sabom, whose work and book is mentioned above, found that a markedly higher percentage of patients who did *not* claim to have undergone a near-death experience than claimed to have them said that they had known about these before their life-threatening events.

None of the theories that has been put forward seems to be convincing. Since there are so many accounts of near-death experiences it is likely that research into them will go on being carried out. For the time being, it would appear that the mind, and perhaps the imagination, or the spirit are exercising a strange power.

Pain and out-of-body experience

Out-of-body experiences do not necessarily involve severe illness or near-death experience. Other factors in life can bring about a condition that is an out-of-body experience without many of the details that characterize near-death experiences.

One of the factors that is claimed to trigger an out-of-body experience is great pain. Reuben Stone in his book *Mysteries of the Mind* (1993) writes of how Odette, the British secret agent during World War II who was captured and tortured by the Gestapo, referred to being able to have out-of-body experiences when the pain of the torture reached a certain level of intensity and became too much to bear. She was able to float above her body and watch her captors at work. Stone refers to the fact that she was then free of physical feelings and so did not feel the excruciating pain that was being inflicted on her.

Other people who claim to have had out-of-body experiences also say that they were in great pain when the experiences occurred. Victims of car accidents who were so badly injured that the pain was virtually intolerable while waiting for the ambulance sometimes speak of suddenly finding themselves looking down upon themselves. They also often comment on seeing other people standing or lying around, other people who were injured, people who were organizing treatment, the po-

lice directing traffic around the accident scene and
ghouls who had stopped to watch.

Victims who have been badly injured or burnt in ex-
plosions or fires have also claimed to have had out-of-
body experiences. They have spoken of remembering
being removed from the crumbling or burning building
on stretchers, feeling agonizing pain and then suddenly
being up above witnessing the scene below, seeing the
firemen and the police trying to deal with the situation.

Stone in *Mysteries of the Mind* writes of Ed Morrell, a
prisoner in the Arizona State Penitentiary, the conditions
in which are considered to be among the toughest in
America. Morrell, who wrote a book about his experiences entitled *The Twenty-fifth Man*, referred to some of
the tortures to which he was subjected. Among the most
savage of these was being tied into two straitjackets and
having water poured over him so that the straitjackets
shrank, causing even more pain. He described such an
experience as like being 'slowly squeezed to death'.

Morrell claims that his way of coping with such agonizing experiences was to undergo out-of-body experiences. In them he not only was able to float out of his
body and look down at his body being racked with pain
but he was able to travel out of his cell around the prison
and further afield. This is sometimes known as 'astral
travel' and is dealt with later in this chapter.

John Spencer in his book *The Paranormal—A Modern
Perspective* (1992) writes about the experience of a
woman, Audrey Bourne, who experienced great pain on

being given an exceptionally unpleasant internal gynae-
cological examination in London in 1984. She claims to
have floated out of her body in the way that other people
have.

Her account, however, is different from those that
have already been discussed. In other accounts the people claiming to have had out-of-body experiences have
seen themselves lying down or at least inactive.

Audrey Bourne described how she saw herself walking along the street and crossing the road, taking all the
usual precautions.

As Spencer points out, this raises an interesting point
about the body that is left behind in an out-of-body experience. If the body is simply lying on a bed and not
doing anything active, then it is a fair assumption, if you
believe in any of this at all, that it does not need the
mind, or astral body, which is supposedly up above
looking down on the body.

However, in the case of Audrey Bourne it appears that
her body was still going around doing its usual things
and presumably she would have needed her mind to help
her cross a busy road. Either the mind, or astral body,
was still controlling the body from above or some of the
mind had been left behind, if Audrey Bourne's account
of her out-of-body experience is to be believed.

Thus, claimed out-of-body experiences seem often to
be a response to pain. In several cases, indeed, it seems
to be a way for the people who are being subjected to
pain to free themselves from that pain. As we have seen

earlier in this chapter some people do claim to be able to bring on out-of-body experiences at will. A particularly painful experience would obviously be a good time to do this, if it were in fact possible.

Reverie and out-of-body experience

Not all those who claim to have had out-of-body experiences have had them in response to pain. Some speak of having them in response to boredom. I have heard accounts of people who were so bored at work that they were sitting staring into space when they had the sensation of floating out of themselves and finding themselves looking down at themselves still sitting at their desks—and still staring into space.

Perhaps this is a skill that we should all try to cultivate. It would be an excellent way of getting out of excessively boring meetings without actually leaving the room bodily and so appearing rude.

I personally know someone who used to experience great periods of blankness when she was suffering from depression. As is quite common in depression, she would be in the middle of some task and she would suddenly come to to find that she had been staring blankly into space for some minutes, the task undone or unfinished.

On one or two such occasions she would find herself floating upwards and then looking down on herself, still staring into space rather than completing the task. The person who described these experiences, which happened a number of years ago, had not heard of the term out-of-body experiences but she would have appeared to have undergone them.

A feeling of relaxation has led to some claimed cases of out-of-body experience. People have spoken of having undergone such an experience when they have been lying on a sofa, listening to music and thinking of nothing much in a state of pleasant relaxation.

Others report having undergone out-of-body experiences as a result of drug-taking. In *Mysteries of the Mind*, referred to earlier in the chapter, Reuben Stone refers to research conducted by a Dr Charles Tart, a psychologist. In 1971 Tart carried out a survey of 150 regular smokers of marijuana and discovered that 44 per cent of them had had an out-of-body experience while under the influence of the drug. This is significantly higher than figures given for the general population, although these vary considerably, as has been pointed out earlier in this chapter.

Out-of-body experiences at will

It is claimed by some that out-of-body experiences can be induced at will with a bit of practice. One suggested way given in *The Projection of the Astral Body* (1992) written by Sylvan Muldoon is to make sure that you are thirsty before you go to bed, to go to sleep while you are imagining that you are going to the kitchen to get a drink of water and telling yourself to wake up out of your body when you are at the sink.

In *The Paranormal—A Modern Perspective*, John Spencer writes of advice given by Robert Monroe who claims to have trained himself to have out-of-body experiences and to go on astral travel. He lists a few guidelines, some of which resemble advice given to achieve meditation.

I would not personally recommend this. For my own part I think that I shall just wait for an out-of-body experience to occur naturally.

However, there do seem to be people, often people who claim that they are psychic, who can induce out-of-body experiences at will. Such people have been used in research of the kind carried out by Dr Charles Tart, mentioned above.

Astral travel

In what is sometimes known as astral travel, the person who claims to have had an out-of-body experience claims not to have remained in the space above his or her body but to have travelled around the area and even much further afield. This is said to have happened in the case of Ed Morrell, described above under 'Pain and out-of-body experiences'.

Other people have spoken of finding themselves travelling over towns and cities, looking down on the rooftops and the scenes below. Some people who have had out-of-body experiences when they have been lying on their beds with nothing much to do have spoken of having had out-of-body experiences that involved trav-

elling around the hospital and even listening into con-
versations.

Reuben Stone in *Mysteries of the Mind* refers to a
claim made by the American medium, Eileen Garrett, in
her autobiography that she succeeded in having an out-
of-body experience in which she 'visited' a doctor who
lived in Newfoundland from New York where she herself lived. She claims to have observed that the doctor
had a bandage on his head and to have noted a number of
different objects on the doctor's table.

On returning to New York and her body Garrett wrote
down details of things that she had noticed and posted
them to the doctor. He in turn sent a telegraph confirm-
ing the accuracy of her report.

Strange indeed and stranger still because the doctor
had in fact asked Garrett to 'visit' him. Indeed he claims
to have known that she was there and even opened a
book so that she could read a page.

Remote viewing

It is difficult to explain this, if the account is true. Stone
points out that Garrett was held to be exceptionally psychic, being one of the most accomplished mediums that
has ever been and that the Newfoundland doctor was
also psychic. He suggests that Garrett's 'visit' may have
been an example of 'remote viewing' or 'travelling
clairvoyance' and that it was not her mind, spirit or astral body that was there but that she was there psychically.

Remote viewing is described by Betty Shine in her book *Mind Waves* (1993). In it she describes how she was able to 'visit' her family when she was evacuated from London during World War II and was living in a fairly remote place feeling lonely and homesick. She was able to picture herself sitting at the fire and seeing and smelling cakes.

Later, after much practice, she was able to become skilled in the art of remote viewing. She tells of how she and her daughter, when they were living in a remote part of Spain, were able to let their minds travel to the nearest village to 'see' what their friends were doing.

She castigates scientists for their 'pathetic' explanations of 'remote viewing' and says that it is because their own minds are closed they cannot undergo multidimensional experiences or begin to understand them. In her description of remote viewing, Shine speaks of gaining control over mind energy and of reaching an understanding that 'the mind can and does travel'.

Summary
It is probably difficult for most of us even to begin to understand remote viewing. However, it is equally difficult to ignore the whole question of out-of-body experiences or, even more, to ignore the whole question of near-death experiences. There have been so many reported and documented cases that it seems hard to believe that there is absolutely nothing in the phenomena of out-of-body experiences and near-death experiences, even if

we are nowhere near to understanding how they come about.

Perhaps science one day will come up with some answers, reasons and causes. Until then we are faced with the thought that the mind is so powerful that it can detach itself from the body, possibly still leaving some form of mind control with the physical body so that it can still function.

Chapter 6

Psychokinesis

Psychokinesis is the apparent ability by someone to influence other people, objects or events by an effort of will and not involving any known physical force. In other words the human mind is claimed to be able to influence people, objects and events by a direction of will. Some people seem to have the ability to manipulate the physical world by the sheer power of their minds. Psychokinesis is sometimes called either telekinesis or 'mind over matter'.

Metal-bending
An example of supposed psychokinesis that had a great deal of media attention in relatively recent times was metal-bending. In this the person claiming to have the gift of psychokinesis tries to bend metal objects without exerting any force on them. If the metal bends the claim is that it will have been the power of the person's mind that has brought this about.

Metal-bending is not new. Scientists such as Faraday were researching the phenomenon in the 1850s and other scientists have done so over the years. Perhaps one thing that has changed since the early years of metal-bending is that supposedly successful cases of it used sometimes to be ascribed to a spirit rather than to the mind of the person involved in the metal-bending.

Noted cases of claimed metal-bending include the feats of Joe Mangini of Columbia, Missouri who is said to have bent cutlery that had been sealed inside a bottle so there was no possibility that Mangini could have physically touched it directly.

Geller

The fact that people today are familiar with the phenomenon of metal-bending, if not with the word psychokinesis, is largely due to Uri Geller. In the 1970s he began to demonstrate publicly and worldwide his claimed powers to be able to bend metal objects, such as spoons, without exerting force on them and to be able to perform other extraordinary feats involving metal objects

One of the first widely reported demonstration of his claimed ability occurred on 23 November 1973 when he appeared as a guest on a television show broadcast by the BBC. The show was The David Dimbleby Talk-In.

Geller performed a whole range of feats. He rubbed two broken watches and made them work again. He also made the hands of one of the said watches bend upwards inside the glass of the watch without touching the hands. A fork held by David Dimbleby was stroked by Geller and it bent. Moreover, a fork that was lying on the table in the studio between Dimbleby and his guest began to bend.

The metal objects bent or otherwise affected by Geller

impressed many people, even people who were sceptical
as to how he had succeeded in performing the feats.
What was also impressive and extremely surprising was
the fact that a considerable number of people had
phoned the BBC during the show to say that some of the
forks and spoons in their houses had become bent by
themselves in the course of the show. Others spoke of
clocks that had been stopped for years beginning to
chime and of objects that seemed to move of their own
accord.

Geller's exploits became very popular and they became the centre of a huge controversy. Some magicians
claimed that Geller's feats could all be performed by
stage magicians and were nothing to do with psychokinesis—Geller had been performing as an amateur conjuror when he was first discovered. Others said that such
tricks could certainly not be performed by stage magicians, that they had nothing whatsoever to do with
sleight of hand.

According to some scientists, one of the problems
with deciding the truth about Geller is that there is a
shortage of evidence from controlled studies or of scientific experiments relating to his supposed psychokinetic
ability. He became swamped in the razzmatazz of the
media circus too soon for that.

Two accounts of non-stage feats by Geller, however,
seem unusual. One of these is reported in *Mysteries of
the Mind* (1993) by Reuben Stone. One of these concerns an incident that occurred when he was on his first

trip to America in 1972. The other concerns Big Ben, the famous clock in London.

When he was in America he met the American astronaut, Edgar G. Mitchell, who had been on the Apollo 14 moon mission and who had tried to carry out some ESP experiences from space. Geller had lunch with Mitchell and Mitchell's secretary, as well as a psychical researcher and a physicist.

Geller is said to have asked Mitchell's secretary to remove a gold ring which she was wearing and to cup it in the closed palm of her hand. He then moved his hand backwards and forwards over the woman's hand without touching it.

Gerald Feinberg, who was the physicist present, is said to have reported that the woman opened her hand and it was seen that the ring in it had a crack in it as though it had been cut by an extremely sharp instrument. The physicist also reported that in the course of a few hours the ring became twisted and gradually formed itself into the shape of an 'S'.

Such a phenomenon in some circumstances might have been the result of sleight of hand in that another ring might have been put in place of the original one. In these circumstances where there were independent witnesses, one of whom was a scientist and so presumably reasonably sceptical about paranormal activity, it is difficult to see how this could have happened.

A later example of his seeming power was demonstrated when Geller was asked by an American games company to stop Big Ben at midnight on New Year's Eve 1989/1990 as evidence of his claimed talent. Geller has written proof that the games company approached him in this way.

By this time Geller was living in England and decided to go to Westminster, where Big Ben is located, on 17 December, the day after he had agreed to take up the company's challenge, in order to experiment ahead of the day of the challenge. He arrived about midday, and Big Ben is recorded as having stopped at 12.35 p.m.

It is extremely difficult to account for this in ordinary rational terms. Security at Westminster is naturally extremely tight and vigilant, and it would be virtually impossible for Geller to have engaged an accomplice to interfere with the clock. Coincidence is always a possibility in such cases but in this case it seems rather a remote possibility. Geller was present when the clock stopped and he had written proof of the company's challenge.

Geller took part in several challenges to give a very public demonstration of his claimed psychokinetic power. One of these took place when he was on the ship *Renaissance* travelling between Spain and Italy. Some of the members of the ship's band thought it would be amusing to challenge Geller to stop the ship.

Immediately Geller took up the challenge and very shortly afterwards people became aware that the ship was beginning to lose power. When the ship's engines died the engineers found that the cause of the trouble was a crimped fuel line, fuel lines being made of metal.

Some people claimed that this was just coincidence and, of course, incredible coincidences do occur. However it would be an amazing coincidence if the ship's metal fuel line developed a kink when someone noted for his ability to bend metal had just taken up a challenge to stop the ship.

Apparently the time between the challenge being issued and Geller beginning to concentrate on the challenge was too short for Geller to have got an accomplice to damage the fuel line, even if he had had a companion who was knowledgeable enough about ships. This seems unlikely.

Geller has many detractors and he has many admirers. Perhaps the truth about his supposed gift may never be known. Given that some of his feats do seem too extraordinary to have a simple rational explanation it seems likely that he does have some kind of strange ability. For example, an electron microscope study of a key bent by Geller indicated that its metal structure had been rearranged and that the break showed characteristics other than those of a key broken by ordinary means.

However, the authors, Hans J. Eysenck and Carl Sargent, of the book *Explaining the Unexplained* write, 'It seems clear now that Geller has been observed and recorded enhancing any PK (psychokinetic) ability he may possess by sleight of hand.' It could be that he does have some genuine powers but that in some cases these have been made to produce even more astonishing effects than would otherwise have been the case.

Hasted

Another famous name in psychokinesis is John Hasted, but he is not noted for his metal-bending or for any other supposedly psychokinetic ability. He is a scientist. While professor of physics at Birbeck College, London, he has done a great deal of research into supposed psychokinetic ability.

He has come up with some rather amazing findings. Some of the subjects whom he was investigating were able to make paper clips form tangled clusters although no one was touching them at the time and although they were enclosed in a glass ball.

Hasted, working with schoolchildren in the 1980s, produced some convincing results. In 1982 one of the schoolboys involved in these experiments, Mark Briscoe, succeeded in putting a piece of wire made of nitriol permanently out of shape by stroking it.

This was extremely surprising since nitriol has the peculiar property of being able permanently to hold its shape. The only way it can be reshaped permanently is to subject it under tension to great heat, at temperatures of 900 degrees. At least that was thought to have been the only way until Mark Briscoe came along.

Hasted also carried out psychokinetic tests using a bar made of a brittle alloy that cannot be bent to a particular angle of deformation in less than a specified time. Should undue force be applied to try to speed up this process the bar will break. Hasted has reported the bending of such a bar by one of his subjects in significantly less time than the specified minimum time.

Gauges were also used by Hasted in his research. For example, he attached metal objects to gauges that would test strain and to recording instruments. Even although no one touched the objects, the recording instruments recorded stress readings.

It is obvious that Hasted conducted his experiments with a very open mind, without the prejudice that many scientists show towards anything that is suggestive of the paranormal. Indeed, he is on record as having said that PK (psychokinesis) worked better if the psychological attitude of everyone concerned with the experiment was positive rather than negative and if everyone was in a relaxed state.

Human nature being what it is, it is likely that many of us will find ourselves more inclined to believe a scientist than we would someone who started out as an amateur conjuror. We are likely, therefore, to view Hasted's work with less scepticism than we view that of Geller. Even given this bias, the experiments carried out by Hasted seem impressive and would appear to suggest that some minds are capable of some kind of influence over metal objects

Crussard and Bouvaist

Crussard and Bouvaist are French researchers who have worked in the field of psychokinesis. They too have come up with some astonishing results.

They have recorded incidents in which the French

metal-bender Jean-Paul Girard succeeded in bending metal strips that were encased in sealed glass tubes. Hasted and other researchers examined the results and the methods used to obtain them and came to the conclusion that the possibility of fraud could be excluded.

The French researchers have also recorded experiments with Girard using aluminium strips, which have resulted in changes to the strips that would not normally have appeared except at exceptionally high temperatures. These changes are not visible to the naked eye but are detectable only by metallurgical analysis.

As is the case with Hasted, the work of the researchers does seem to have a ring of truth about it. Perhaps we are being blinded by science but it is difficult to ignore or be sceptical about experiments that indicate actual physical changes in metal.

Moving objects

Metal-bending is not the only instance of supposed psychokinetic ability that has attracted attention in relatively recent times. Some people claim not be able to bend objects but to be able to move them by the force of their minds without touching the objects.

For example, Alla Vinogravada from Moscow in the 1970s is said to have made objects weighing up to three ounces roll across a table top without her or anyone else touching them. She is also said to have been able to make objects about a third lighter than that slide across a surface.

Kulagina

Reuben Stone in *Mysteries of the Mind* draws our attention to someone who seems to have demonstrated psychokinetic ability a few years before Geller made the headlines. The someone in question is Nelya, or Nina, Kulagina, a former Red Army sergeant.

She did not enjoy the media success of Geller and so few of us are likely to have heard of her, especially since relations between the West and what was then Russia were not so open as they later became. Unlike Geller, she was not noted for her metal-bending prowess but for her seeming ability to cause objects to move.

Kulagina first attracted the notice of researchers because of her ability to detect the colours of sewing threads simply by touching them and because she appeared to be able to 'read' a newspaper by running her fingertips over the paper. In the course of their research into these strange powers of hers some of the researchers noticed that any small object that was near her fingertips when she was practising her powers would move without anyone or anything touching it.

It was not only metal objects that acted like this in the presence of Kulagina. It was noted by some American researchers who went to Russia to study her powers that she could affect objects made of a whole range of materials including plastic, paper and fabric as well as metal.

The objects never seemed to move very far—a box of matches, for example, is said to have moved three inches— and it is claimed that they varied in their rate of progress. Some moved smoothly and slowly while others moved jerkily in fits and starts.

Kulagina does seem to have been extremely closely monitored by researchers, particularly by the American researchers, and so it is difficult to see how fraud can have been involved. In addition, it would appear that her supposed powers to move objects came to light only accidentally when it was discovered that small objects automatically moved away from her when she was using her fingertips instead of her eyes to 'see' things.

One of Kulagina's great skills was her ability to deflect a compass needle. This she was able to do in full view of the camera.

Perhaps here we shall have to give the mind some credit for being able to influence inanimate objects until we find out otherwise. We shall have to wait and see what science comes up with by way of rational, non-paranormal explanation.

Levitation
There are two kinds of levitation. One of these relates to the rising of one's own body. However, it is the other meaning that interests us here. Levitation can also apply to the rising into the air of objects supposedly as a result of someone's psychokinetic powers.

Kulagina, whose supposed powers are described above, was also said by Russian researchers to be able to make a ping-pong ball levitate, and she is seen supposedly doing this on a film made by them.

In 1984 a Polish teenager, Joasia Gajewski, seems to have succeeded in making a fork rise and fly across the room as Japanese TV cameramen witnessed the event. Another of her supposed paranormal skills was to make lightbulbs explode at will.

A compatriot of Gajewski, Stanislawa Tomczyk, had supposed powers of levitation in the 1920s. Her speciality was the levitation of scissors.

D. D. Home

Daniel Dunglas Home was born in Edinburgh in 1833 and taken to America in the 1840s. There he became one of the best-known mediums at a time when America was in the grip of Spiritualism and a huge number of people wished to attend seances.

Home is said to have been psychic from an early age and claimed to be in regular contact with the spirits of the dead. There were many other mediums in America at the time, some of whom were undoubtedly leaping on the bandwagon of the Spiritualist movement. Home's seances were particularly popular, partly because of the variety of physical effects that seemed to occur at his sessions. People spoke of hearing rapping and of being gripped by unseen hands. There was also talk of levitation both of Home himself, of other people and of objects in the room.

Adare

There are tales of cloths rising from tables and of tables

themselves rising. Glasses were said to rise and fly round the room. The levitation of tables in Home's seances was documented by Lord Adare, who was a former foreign correspondent with the *Daily Telegraph*. As a journalist he was used to recording details, and he wrote down details of many of Home's seances immediately after they were over. His records indicate that he witnessed sixteen levitations of tables, several of them being extremely heavy.

Crookes

Another witness of levitations of objects at Home's seances was Sir William Crookes, a distinguished physicist. He decided to try to undertake controlled experiments on the levitation effects connected with Home. He reported seeing Home levitating a chair with a woman sitting on it. Another of his reports seems very strange indeed.

Home was fond of music, and he had an accordion that was said to levitate and to go around the room playing 'Home Sweet Home'. In order to find out in what way, if any, Home was involved, Crookes bought an accordion and sealed it in a locked cage. However, that accordion, too, levitated and, although it could not move around the room, it did move around the cage, playing tunes all the time.

As has been pointed out already, Home is said to have been able to levitate himself and even to levitate other people. Even stranger is the fact that he is reported to have been able to elongate his body. There were apparently many witnesses to these occurrences. He is supposed to have on occasion added as much as six inches to his height.

Some of the reports of levitation in relation to Home seem extraordinary and even amusing. Yet they have been testified to by witnesses, and witnesses who seem extremely credible at that and who wrote contemporaneous accounts at the time of, or just immediately after, the relevant seance.

There were many people who were sceptical about Home, and he made many enemies, some of whom, like Robert Browning, said that he was a fraud, but this was never proved, despite the number of people who would have dearly wished to do so. Although Crookes tried to persuade scientists to test Home and do research on his seances and the events, none of them would agree to do so, perhaps because they were rather nervous.

The strange experiences recorded at the seances have been put down by some to hallucination, perhaps brought on by hypnosis. However, not many people are so susceptible to hypnosis that they will hallucinate upon suggestion. In addition, Home's seances were usually conducted in bright light, which is not conducive to hallucination.

Because of the seeming reliability of the witnesses who left written accounts of the activity surrounding Home it is difficult to explain it away. If he was not a complete fraud, and this was not proved, and if mass hallucination does not seem likely at least in all cases, then what was behind the levitation?

No one else seems to have been able to produce these effects on the scale Home did and so perhaps it was some strange power of his mind that caused the levitation and other phenomena. Unless someone else who is surrounded by the same effects comes along we are unlikely ever to know and even then we might still be left in the dark.

Summary

Dismissing all of claimed psychokinesis as fraud, sleight of hand or hallucination is tempting to the sceptic but in some cases there seems to be actual evidence, as is the case with some claimed metal-bending instances, that something strange has happened that cannot be explained by any normal means. It does seem possible, however unlikely it may seem, that a human mind can affect inanimate objects in some way

Chapter 7

The Mind's Role in Illness and Health

Despite the phenomenal progress that has been made in medicine, it is still widely acknowledged that the mind can play a significant part in our state of health. It can have a role in our becoming ill and a role in our recovery.

The Mind and Illness

Resistance to disease

Folk medicine and popular literature have always assumed that if people are in some way below par emotionally or mentally they are more likely to become ill. We have all heard stories of young women who went into what used to be called 'a decline' after they were parted from their lovers, whether because of death, desertion or parental intervention. The decline was not only a state of depression or lowered spirits but an actual physical decrease in energy, health and wellbeing, sometimes even ending in death.

Many of us witness a less dramatic form of this in ourselves. If we are feeling down we seem to pick up a whole series of colds and minor ailments, but if we are in top form we seem to be able to avoid these, even though we may be in contact with people who have them. It is as though our state of mind has affected our immune system.

SAD

Simply the fact that it is winter and that there is less light about about than usual can put some of us into such a depressed state, known as Seasonal Affective Disorder and often abbreviated to SAD, that we seem to get a whole series of winter ailments. People suffering from seasonal affective disorder find that they want to sleep far longer than they usually do and speak of having very little energy or enthusiasm for life.

Many animals become inactive in winter and some hibernate until spring comes around. Some scientists believe that in people suffering from SAD there may be a trigger in the brain similar to that of animals that slows them down.

Light would appear to have a therapeutic effect on seasonal affective disorder. Sufferers have spoken of a huge improvement in their condition if they sit in front of a bank of full-spectrum fluorescent lamps for some time each day.

Life events

Other circumstances that seem to be able to lower our resistance to infection and disease include unfortunate life events, such as death and divorce, and also life events that seem to be either neutral events, such as moving house, or even happy events, such as getting married or having a baby. It seems that if an event causes a major change in our lives then our resistance to disease and infection can be affected for the worse.

This is why we commonly hear accounts of people who become ill after the death of a close relative. This situation often occurs when a spouse dies after a long marriage, even in cases where the marriage has not been a happy one. The survivor does not seem to be able to get over the death or to be able to cope alone, although survivor and deceased may not have seemed inseparable or dependent on each other when the deceased was alive. Such a reaction can manifest itself either in the onset of a new illness or in the exacerbation of an existing one.

Sometimes the person succeeds in shaking off the illness after some considerable time, in the way that people can come out of a period of depression without having been given any form of treatment. In other cases, however, this is not the case, and it is by no means unusual for someone who may have been ill, but certainly not terminally ill, to die not long after the deceased spouse. It is as if the survivor just gave up the desire to live.

This lack of will is sometimes seen by doctors in patients who are told that they have something seriously wrong with them. There are many who decide to get on with life as well as they can for as long as they can. There are others, however, who suddenly get worse after having been told the news of their condition and may even die long before they would have been expected to do so, given the nature and prognosis of their condition. They seem to lose the will to live on being given the information about their illness, often some form of cancer, and appear to decide simply to turn their heads to the wall and die.

The attitude of mind of such people seems to have significantly affected their physical condition. It is as though their mental states were communicated to their bodies and affected their states of health.

Immune system

Many of the accounts we hear of people simply turning their heads to the wall and dying are anecdotal—stories we have heard from a friend of a friend, rather than accounts of which we have hard proof. Nevertheless, many doctors and scientists now believe that there can be a marked connection between a person's mental or emotional state and the state of his or her body, perhaps between a state of mind and the immune system.

Scientists have recently begun to place more credence on the latter possibility, and there is now a branch of brain research, known as psychoneuroimmunology, that deals with finding a correlation between state of mind and the immune system. Until quite recently the immune system was regarded as being a system of defence that acted independently of the brain and hormone systems, but scientists have uncovered some evidence that suggests that the brain does exert some influence on the immune system, thereby giving some credibility to the fact that one's state of mind can decrease one's immunity to disease. Thus, two people could be told at the same time that they have an incurable disease and one of these might die within a very short time while the other might live for the expected time or even longer.

Even more exciting recent research suggests that animals, and thus possibly people, can learn to suppress their own immune system. If this did prove to be the case it would be extremely good news for anyone suffering from an auto-immune disease in which the sufferer's immune system gets it wrong and begins to attack the tissues of the body that it is meant to be defending and protecting. Unfortunately, early research suggests that the major effects on the immune system tend to be suppressive and so negative. However, this kind of research is still in its infancy.

All this research, although at an early stage, does suggest that there is some scientific evidence for the fact that people who are generally at a low ebb emotionally or mentally tend to get more ailments or diseases than they would if they were in a more cheerful, energetic frame of mind. The fact has been the subject of anecdotal evidence for hundreds of years, but there are some sceptics who always need things proved scientifically.

Anorexia

There is one condition, distressingly common in modern

times particularly among girls and young women, in which there is a very obvious connection between the mind and physical state. The condition is anorexia nervosa, otherwise known simply as anorexia.

In this condition it is not a question of an attitude of mind leading someone to become more ill than he or she need be and even to die. It is a question of people's perceptions of themselves leading them, wrongly, to think that they are fat, ugly and disgusting and then leading them to deprive their bodies of food and vital nutrients so that they become ill and even die.

They look in the mirror and see through their minds' eyes enormous people reflected back at them while other people look at them and see very thin or emaciated people. Their minds are causing them to look at themselves in a completely wrong way, which leads them to be very low in self-esteem.

That the condition of anorexia has become more common in recent decades has been put down to the image of the ideal woman, someone almost unbelievably slim, that fashion designers and the media project. Then there are the young women, thin often to the point of emaciation, who parade along the fashion show catwalks.

These are obviously contributory factors, but the problem lies in the sufferer's mind, a mind in which self-esteem is very low. It is not the usual form of mental disorder, however, that might have an incidental effect on the state of the body, but one that has a direct effect on the physical state of the body since the mind is indicating that the body should be deprived of nutrition so that a slim enough form can be achieved.

Menstrual irregularity

In many ways the wonder is that the average monthly menstrual cycle is so regular. The monthly pattern is controlled by a mixture of hormones, although the precise nature of that control is not yet fully understood.

Some deviation from what is regarded as a normal cycle, roughly twenty-eight days, although this can vary a bit, can possibly be put down to some kind of hormonal imbalance. There are situations regarding the menstrual cycle, however, in which the mind would seem to play a part.

For example, if a woman or girl is worrying about being pregnant it is quite common for her next menstrual period to be late, not because she is in fact pregnant but seemingly because of her anxiety. It would appear that the mind has intervened and caused chaos.

On the other hand, sometimes women experience a delay in their periods when they are very anxious to become pregnant but in fact turn out not to be so. They are often devastated when their period appears, since they have begun to be convinced that they are pregnant. Again the mind would appear to have had some influence on the menstrual cycle.

It is not only fear of, or a desire for, pregnancy that seems to be able to involve the mind in the menstrual cycle. Any major source of worry or anxiety, such as important examinations or any major change such as a house-moving, seems to have the same effect.

Stress

Our modern lifestyle has led to another condition that can lead the mind to affect the state of the body. The condition is stress, and it has come to be one of the key-words of the closing decades of the twentieth century. The pace of modern life, the competitive dog-eat-dog nature of modern life, heavy workloads and long hours, the insecurity of employment in modern life—all these have been blamed for life becoming more stressful and people becoming more stressed.

Stress can affect the mind. It can make us have difficulty in concentrating, in that a piece of work that would normally have taken us about ten minutes to do can take several hours. Memory, too, can seem to deteriorate, in that we can find ourselves forgetting to do things that would once have seemed like second nature or forgetting telephone numbers that we would once have been able to reel off without thinking.

Our mood can also be affected. Instead of being relatively cheerful and easy-going, we are made irritable and aggressive by stress, a change that can have adverse effects on our relationships with other people. Stress can also markedly reduce our energy levels so that we are tired and fatigued all the time.

A more surprising fact is that stress seems to be able to produce physical disorders and illnesses, as though our minds were trying to tell us that if we want to remain well we must change our lifestyle. A wide range of disorders are now frequently ascribed to stress.

Fight or flight

Our early ancestors also could have been said to suffer from stress, but it was a different kind. They would have had to worry about being attacked by predators, finding enough food, keeping warm, all the basics of life.

In such a situation the brain helps the body cope. The brain identifies a situation as being potentially problematic or dangerous and sends a message down to our nervous system to adjust our physical functions to enable us to deal with the situation. To increase our energy levels we produce more adrenaline in the bloodstream. Our heart rate increases markedly, our blood pressure rises, our muscles become tense and our breathing becomes more shallow. Our brain has seen to it that we are ready to fight a problematic or dangerous situation.

This was the kind of mechanism that helped our ancestors survive, a mechanism that prepared them automatically for 'fight or flight' in the face of danger. The same mechanism still comes to our aid if we are in sudden physical danger. If you are in a burning building you will race for the nearest exit, if a runaway car is heading towards you, you will throw yourself out of its path, if someone attacks you, you will either run away or hit back, according to the circumstances and your personality type.

The problem is that, although we are rarely in much physical danger, we are frequently in what to us are stressful situations—indeed, for some of us life is one unremitting period of stress from which we cannot seem to switch off. Instead of occasionally requiring the help of our 'fight or flight' mechanism, we make constant demands on it. We practically always have an excess of adrenaline, our heart rate is rarely slow, our blood pressure is frequently high, our muscles practically always tense and our breathing almost always shallow. Our brain is constantly getting our body functions into overdrive and getting us ready for a 'fight or flight' response although there is not usually an element of actual physical activity in our problems.

Inevitably the bodily machinery intended for the occasional crisis becomes confused and begins to break down when it is facing constant demands. It is at this point that stress-induced disorders can occur.

It should be pointed out here that it is not the pace of modern life, heavy workloads or a high degree of competitiveness that leads to stress but our individual attitudes to these. Some people simply shrug them off as part of life, some positively enjoy what they see as a challenge while others become stressed.

In addition it is not unusual for people's attitudes to change towards the conditions of modern living according to their circumstances. The happy, trouble-free bachelor who revels in the challenges thrown at him in a cut-throat business world can readily become stressed a few years later if he acquires a great many financial commitments and some children and is worrying about job security.

The fact is that many people present themselves at doctors' surgeries with physical symptoms that seem to have been caused by stress. Indeed scientists and doctors have known since the early 1950s that stress was a likely causal factor in several diseases.

One of the most likely of these disorders is heart trouble, and another one, and one that can lead to heart trouble, is hypertension or raised blood pressure. Headaches, too, are often stress-related, although these can either be directly stress-related or be the result of high blood pressure. Stressed individuals often complain of breathlessness, which can either be directly stress-related or be a result of heart trouble. Others again complain of rapid heart rate, excessive sweating, excessive flushing or panic attacks

Most of these disorders are signs that the 'fight or flight' mechanism has gone into overdrive but has been misdirected and has led to problems. Some experts believe that certain personality types, namely high-achieving, ambitious people known as 'type A' personalities, are more likely to suffer some of the possible results of excessive stress, such as heart attacks.

Some stress-related disorders seem less obviously related to confusion in the 'fight or flight' mechanism. These include the falling out of hair, which can be a source of embarrassment as well as concern, particularly in women. The skin can also be involved. Rashes and bouts of eczema also seem to be stress-related in some cases.

Thus stress is not just a matter of feeling that you are unable to cope, of being unable to relax or switch off, of feeling anxious all the time, of being unable to sleep, of eating too little or too much, or of drinking too much alcohol to try to forget your problems. It can manifest itself physically in the form of some kind of illness or disorder.

Counselling

More and more concern is now being raised about the effects of stress on individuals involved in some particular stressful or traumatic situation. Thus counselling is now often given to people who, in the course of their employment or ordinary lives, encounter a situation that is likely to cause them great distress or stress. This is done in an effort to obviate the worst of the side effects of trauma, known as post-traumatic stress disorder.

People who receive this kind of counselling include firefighters who survive a conflagration in which people, sometimes some of their colleagues, are killed; police officers who witness the death of a colleague at the hands of a gunman; school pupils who are in the same class as a young person who has been murdered; the survivors of some disaster, such as train crash. By getting early counselling it is hoped that the worst effects of stress on the health of such individualscan be mitigated.

It is possible, as seems to be the case in people with

rather a depressed state of mind, that extreme stress may in fact in some way affect the immune system. Thus doctors should really be treating not the disease or the symptoms of the disease but the state of mind that has led to this. Unfortunately, this is easier said than done.

Stress reduction

Various suggestions have been made for the relief of stress. These include physical exercise, relaxation techniques, meditation, yoga, aromatherapy, acupuncture, hypnosis, psychotherapy and counselling, and these are effective in many cases. It is often difficult, however, to convince the stress sufferer to try any of these, particularly when very stressed individuals find it very difficult to relax.

Sometimes the stress symptoms disappear when the person is removed from the situation that is causing the stress, but this is not always the case. In any case, it is not always possible, as people have to earn a living and it is often the work situation that is giving rise to the stress.

Stress certainly seems to make the body of the sufferer less able to protect itself from disease. Extreme forms of stress, such as great shock or sudden, extreme fear, even seem to be able to bring on sudden death without any obvious organic cause.

Despite the various approaches that exist to reduce the effects of stress and so to try to eradicate the symptoms and disease that it can cause, it remains a major health problem. This is true even when stress is identified as the cause of a disorder. Too often, the situation is worse in that general practitioners do not always have the time to get to the bottom of what is really wrong with a patient and frequently simply provide medication for insomnia, skin rashes, or whatever physical form the stress takes. The mind has been at work but this has not been noticed.

Psychosomatic illness

At least it has now been recognized generally by the medical profession that there is such a thing as a stress-related illness, even if all general practitioners do not have the time or even the inclination to spot the signs of this modern condition. This has to be seen as progress.

Not so long ago all stress-related illness would have been dismissed under the blanket term of 'psychosomatic' illness. 'Psychosomatic' means 'concerning the relationship between the mind and the body'. In relation to illness it refers to a physical disease that is psychological in origin, a disease for which there seems to be no physical cause. In other words, a psychosomatic illness is one that is said to be all in the mind, one that is an instance of mind over matter.

Nowadays, as more is known about the cause of some diseases, or as research is being carried out into this, opinions are changing with regard to what was said to be psychosomatic illness. Asthma, for example, used to be said to be a psychosomatic disease but nowadays more physical causes are being researched and identified.

House mites and dust are thought to be very much implicated in the getting of asthma, and research is being carried out into the connection between air pollution and asthma. Certainly, asthma is very much on the increase in modern life as is air pollution. It is generally thought that there may be a psychosomatic element in asthma but this is far from being the whole story.

Eczema, which frequently coexists with asthma, was also formerly assumed to be psychosomatic, but doubts have been raised about this also. Since it often occurs with asthma, it is thought that it might be a skin response to some of the same agents that cause the respiratory disorder. In some cases it is thought to be caused by an allergy to something.

People suffering from severe cases of allergy are often subjected to whole batteries of tests with a view to identifying which substance or substances could be giving rise to the allergies. Given the number of likely substances this can be a lengthy process, and even when a substance is identified life can still be fairly difficult for allergy sufferers since they can end up having to avoid some very common substances such as metal. It is possible that other disorders thought to be psychosomatic might also be a result of allergy.

With reference to such cases, science seems to be going in an opposite direction from the one that it is following in the case of the mind affecting immunity. In the latter, the role of the mind has been demonstrated to be greater, or at least has been demonstrated to exist, while in the former case the mind is seen to be taking a lesser role than was previously thought.

Psychosomatic pain

Formerly a great deal of pain was held to be psychosomatic or 'all in the mind', as people say. It is impossible for someone to say whether or not someone is in pain but a doctor can often say whether or not there is any obvious physical cause of pain, such as a broken limb or damage to a nerve.

Modern diagnostic techniques, such as sophisticated X-ray machines, CT scans and MRI (magnetic resonance imaging), have vindicated many people who might have been said to have been suffering from imaginary pain because one of the diagnostic techniques has revealed a hitherto unexpected physical cause of the pain. Had the diagnostic techniques not been available the pain would have remained categorized as psychosomatic. Here again science has served to reduce the role of the mind as a cause of disorder, in this case pain.

Pain and pain control

People sometimes speak of feeling pain in a part of the body of the kind that they often feel when engaged in some kind of activity at a time when they are not actually engaged in the activity but have been thinking of it. Thus, a dancer may feel pain in a foot that is often painful when a particular step is performed when she is not actually dancing but is simply thinking of performing such a step.

Likewise an athlete such as hurdler might feel pain in his or her legs when thoughts of a race or training come into the mind. The mind associates the action that is thought of with pain and produces the pain.

People who claim to experience such pain say that it seems just as real and feels just as sore as the pain experienced in exercise.

A similar mind-inspired pain has been claimed by some people who have not themselves experienced any form of injury or physical trauma but who have close relatives who have. Some have claimed, for example, that they have experienced severe back pain when close relatives were undergoing surgery, whether or not they knew about the surgery. Others have spoken of having severe unexplained pains in the chest with no seeming cause, only to find a close relative has had a heart attack.

A common example of this is the husband or partner who claims to experience labour pains when his spouse or partner is in the process of giving birth. Some claim to have experienced such pains when they have been away from home at the time of birth and did not know that it was taking place.

As mentioned previously, there are also reported cases of twins feeling each other's pain. For example one twin might feel a searing pain in a leg if his or her twin has sustained a badly injured leg in car or train accident.

Some of this might have to do with what is known as

ESP, or extrasensory perception. More information on this is given in Chapter 2, Telepathy.

Phantom limbs and phantom pain

There is another odd kind of pain that appears to be inspired by the mind since there can be no physical cause identified for it. It is the pain sometimes felt in a phantom limb and sometimes known as phantom pain.

A phantom limb is a sensation of a limb that exists after the actual limb is amputated. Amputees speak of thinking that they can feel some kind of pressure on a leg that has been amputated when the stump has been touched. Others feel a tingling or mild to relatively severe pain in the place where the amputated limb would have been.

People who are born with a limb missing or who have had a limb removed early in childhood do not tend to have this sensation of a phantom limb. It is thought that they do not experience a phantom limb because they have never formed a self image of themselves with their limbs intact. On the other hand, people who have been used to having their limbs intact have a self-image of themselves like that and find it difficult to re-fashion their self-image without a limb.

Whatever the explanation, there can be no physical explanation for feeling as though the limb is still there or for the tingling or the pain. It is surely a case in which the mind is in charge.

Pain is a feeling of discomfort that can vary to a great

extent in intensity. Also some people seem to be able to tolerate greater degrees of pain than others in a similar situation. We say that such people have a greater threshold of pain since the point at which they begin to experience pain is higher than that at which other people begin to feel it.

The ability to feel pain is vital to our safety and survival. A few people are born with a congenital insensitivity to pain and this puts them in terrible danger of doing severe damage to themselves. For example they can badly burn themselves or break bones without being aware of it. Because they do not feel pain they do not instinctively know to avoid some physically dangerous situations that might lead to their deaths.

In ordinary people who feel pain the brain converts nerve impulses into pain. There are two main nerve pathways available for signals from the nerve fibres that receive the pain stimulus. One pathway sends signals extremely rapidly, the other more slowly.

This explains why we often feel the pain from an injury in two waves. We frequently feel at first a short sharp stab of localized pain, courtesy of the signal that has gone by the fast route and then a deep, throbbing longer-lasting and more diffuse pain, courtesy of the signal that has gone by the slower route. The destination of the signals is the thalamus of the brain, which registers the signals and labels them as being painful and the message of pain is then routed to the cerebral cortex near the front of the brain.

There would appear to be an extent to which people can suppress pain, as though their minds were telling their bodies to ignore or be unaware of pain. People who have been shot or who have received some sudden injury, such as a machine cutting off a foot or a limb say that they did not immediately feel pain, that pain did not occur until later, after the initial shock had worn off. Those who have witnessed such traumatic injuries have said that the injured people did not at first cry out in pain and in some cases did not speak of pain until considerably later.

Likewise, in wartime people have spoken of the very severe injuries that soldiers have sustained in battle and yet not referred to any form of pain until several hours later. Doctors have spoken of the fact that soldiers suffering injuries that they have just sustained in battle seem to be able to tolerate them without morphine or other painkillers, unlike civilians suffering similar injuries in different circumstances.

In such cases it seems unlikely that people are simply tolerating high levels of pain. It seems much more likely that the pain has been suppressed for a while by the mind.

There are, moreover, situations in which people seem either to be able to tolerate extremely high levels of pain without showing this or else be able to ignore or suppress it. This occurs in dancers, in the performing of certain ballet steps or positions, and in athletes or gymnasts, when they seem to be able to push themselves beyond the level of pain.

Here again the brain is at work. Scientific research suggests that certain parts of the brain produce chemical substances, such as endorphins, which act in the same way as the opiate morphine to suppress or deaden pain. They may work by getting the brain to send messages that halt the progress of messages of pain. Thus the mind, or rather the brain, would appear to have influence over the body as far as pain control is concerned.

It may be this fact that has enabled people in religious rituals or stage shows to lie on beds of nails, walk on hot coals or perform other painful procedures without appearing to suffer any pain. An alternative theory is that such people can meditate to such an extent that they go into such a deep trance that they do not feel pain.

Hypochondriacs

The previous sections have dealt with psychosomatic illness and psychosomatic pain and changing attitudes to them. Chronic hypochondriacs are people who regularly suffer from imaginary illnesses. They frequently suffer from undiagnosed pain and often present at general practitioners' surgeries with a whole range of symptoms, most of which are not visually obvious.

Any mention of the symptoms of someone's illness, any information in a book or magazine about an illness has them imagining the very symptoms that have been described and worrying that they have that very disease. They are actually only exhibiting to an extreme degree a feature that is probably in all of us. If any of us read a medical book of any kind that describes symptoms we often imagine that we have them at the time of reading—this also includes many new medical students.

The difference between most of us and hypochondriacs is that in most of us the thought that we might have the symptoms of all the diseases that we have read about is a passing thought that we dismiss as being fanciful after a short time. Hypochondriacs, however, remain preoccupied with them and often become convinced that they have the diseases.

Mostly these diseases exist only in the mind of the hypochondriac and in a sense he or she is being controlled by his or her mind in this respect. However, it has been suggested that some hypochondriacs have an abnormal sensitivity to certain bodily sensations, such as minor aches and pains, cold, hunger and thirst.

Others have some psychological factor in their condition in that they have good memories of being ill as children when they were coddled and pampered and subconsciously long to return to those days. Yet again some of them seem to be suffering from a form of mental illness.

Whatever the background to the hypochondria that their patients are suffering from the danger for general practitioners is that they may become so used to assuming that a particular hypochondriac's illnesses are all imaginary that they miss a real disease if a hypochondriac develops one. Diseases inspired by the mind and imagination may have been replaced by a genuine bodily one.

Hysteria

More worrying than hypochondria from the point of view of actual physical symptoms is hysteria. Some people have been known to go blind through hysteria and others have developed paralysis in some or all of their limbs. Such conditions often occur as the result of a shock, whether physical or emotional, or a traumatic accident, and sometimes become cured by another shock, blow or accident of some kind.

Hysterical pregnancies also occur when women develop the symptoms of pregnancy but are not actually pregnant. This hysterical pregnancy, also known as phantom pregnancy or pseudocyesis, most commonly occurs in women who are desperately anxious to have children but who are either having difficulty in doing so or who are unable to do so.

The mind seems to be very much in control in cases of hysterical disorders but Sigmund Freud and Josef Breuer, the Austrian psychoanalysts, believed such conditions to be caused by repressed emotions. Breuer's treatment of 'Anna O', as he called his patient to protect her privacy, involved getting her to talk about her past experiences and this led to the development of psychoanalysis.

'Anna O' was 21 in 1880 when she began treatment and was suffering from a variety of hysterical conditions, such as paralysis of the legs and paralysis of the neck muscles. All these were cured by Breuer letting her talk about her life, including any events that might have led to her hysterical conditions. Before that the most common form of treatment for hysteria was hypnosis.

There is another form of hysteria that is not related to illness but is related to minds. It is mass hysteria, a state in which individuals find themselves doing or saying things that would very probably not normally be in character for them to do or say.

They are usually members of a group ,who are in a suggestible state to the extent of being easily brainwashed and are repeatedly exposed to some kind of 'suggestion'. For example, a group of ordinary, law-abiding villagers might turn into a lynch mob if incited to do so by someone who keeps reminding them of what they are expected to do by leading them in some kind of chant or slogan, such as 'Get him! Get him!' or 'Kill him! Kill him!' Their minds seem to be controlled and their actions manipulated either by the leader of the crowd or by the crowd itself, although it has been suggested that people who become involved in mass hysteria are simply giving rein to existing feelings that are usually kept well in check.

A historic example of mass hysteria seems to have occurred in Salem in America in the early 1690s. There, many of the villagers became affected by mass hysteria and accused various people of being witches. A series of trials were set up and about twenty people were found guilty and executed.

Placebo

'Placebo' is Latin for 'I will please' and is a form of totally inactive medication, such as a pill made entirely from sugar. Placebos are sometimes used in drug trials in which some of a group will be given a real drug and some a placebo.

This system does not always prove the effectiveness of a drug, unless the group in question is a very large one indeed, since exceptionally suggestible people who tend to be ruled by their minds are quite likely to feel that they have been cured by something that looks like a pill even if it is entirely harmless and free of medication. It is thought that in any trial group about a third of all patients are found to be what are known as placebo reactors, in other words people who seem to be cured by pills that are entirely medication-free.

For this reason placebos are sometimes given to people who are suffering badly from some imaginary illness. This is done so that they think that they have been given medication to cure an illness that is very real to them, although it is thought not to exist.

Likewise placebos are sometimes given to people who think they cannot live without a prescribed drug that they really do not need any more. If they feel that they are still taking the drug they feel better as though they were still taking it, a case of mind over matter. A placebo is sometimes used in conjunction with psychotherapy.

The placebo effect, as it is known, is based on the belief that the pill that is being taken will have an advantageous or a curative effect on their condition. The effect need not be related to a pill. Anything that suggests to people that it will help or cure a condition might produce such an effect.

For example, it has been shown that if two groups of people suffering from post-dental extractions are given a supposed pain-killing injection that is really only a harmless saline injection and one group has the injection administered by a computer-controlled automatic pump and the other group has it administered by a doctor with a white coat on and a stethoscope round his neck, it is likely that the group that had the injection from the doctor will speak of great relief of pain while the group that had the injection through the agency of the computer will likely speak of little in the way of pain relief. The traditional 'uniform' of a doctor has inspired greater confidence and belief than the computer.

In the case of people who seem to have had their pain or symptoms alleviated by the ministrations of a witch doctor or primitive healer the placebo effect may have been at work. The whole panoply of the ritual involved may have had much the same effect as the white coat and stethoscope of the modern doctor.

Clearly the mind is at work somewhere along the line and once again the scientists are researching this. The response to a placebo may be the result of certain chemicals being released in the brain, in the same way that they are thought to be released to postpone or suppress pain. Whatever the exact facts, the placebo effect is certainly mind-driven or brain-driven.

Summary

These then are some of the ways in which the mind is claimed to be able to affect our physical state for the worse. Modern scientific research seems to back the claims in some cases.

For example, the brain produces a substance that can suppress or delay pain in certain situations. In other cases scientific research has helped to identify a physical cause for a pain or ailment in that medical diagnostic techniques are now much more sophisticated and can detect disorders that would have formerly been put down to the imagination, the mind or hypochondria. Doubtless science will continue to come up with the fruits of new research regarding the brain and our perception of the role of the mind might yet change further.

The Mind and Health

The mind is also held to be able to affect our physical state for the better. It is claimed that it can help to improve our health and sense of wellbeing and improve our chances of recovery if we are ill.

The mind and keeping well

The above section has dealt with illness in relation to the mind and state of mind. Bearing in mind what has been said about the relationship between life events, particularly sad or unfortunate events such as death or divorce, and ill health or even death, it would be a good piece of advice to steer clear of such events. However, clearly this would not be possible unless we locked ourselves away from the world and even then misfortune would almost certainly seek us out.

We just have to accept philosophically that we will receive our full share of sad or unfortunate life events and that these may well effect our physical state. The only thing we can do is to make every effort to recover from the mental and physical effects by any means at our disposal as quickly as possible.

We cannot avoid life events that might have a deleterious affect on our health but we can take such steps are as possible to avoid something else that has a bad effect on our physical health, courtesy of the brain—stress. It is impossible to avoid all stress, and indeed a certain amount of stress is said to be good for us, but we can try to avoid situations that we know will cause us undue stress and so will get our brains to signal our bodies to protest in the form of some kind of illness. Sometimes we have to change our lifestyles completely in order to keep our lives as stress-free as possible and our bodies and minds as well as possible.

Meditation

There are those who feel that we can use our minds to help us stay stress-free and well. They advocate that we harness the power of our minds to help us relax, tension being a close cousin of stress, try out a relaxation programme, meditation or yoga.

Many of us, again, feel that we are the kind of people that simply cannot relax, that we would be bored or that meditation and yoga sound too airy-fairy for such practical people as ourselves. These are quite common views but many people who started off as sceptics tried out relaxation, meditation or yoga and found them helpful.

Concentration to a greater or lesser extent in all of these is an essential part and in all of them the mind plays a significant part, if indeed it is not totally in control. Even in simple relaxation techniques the person intent on relaxing is often asked to concentrate on each part of the body in turn in order to get it to relax.

Meditation has long been an integral part of many Eastern religions as a means of emptying the mind of any distracting thoughts in order to achieve spiritual enlightenment. However, many people in the West now use it, not for any spiritual purpose but as way to achieve complete relaxation, a way to get more in touch with their own minds or explore their subconscious or a way to find inner peace. It is an exacting discipline of the mind requiring you to direct your thoughts on one particular point as well as controlling your breathing and relaxing the various parts of your body.

Yoga also requires mental discipline as well as a degree of suppleness. Here again concentration and the power of the mind are important.

People really skilled in the art of yoga have been known to change their heart rate, lower their body temperature and bring their metabolic system almost to a complete halt. Few of us are likely to achieve such heights but meditation has been shown in some cases to slow the heart rate and respiratory rate and to lower the blood pressure. Once again the mind is affecting our bodily functions.

Be happy

Many people feel that, as well as a healthy diet and a reasonable amount of exercise, a positive state of mind will help to keep us well and that all of us should take steps to bring this about.

It is felt by many that a happy frame of mind can keep us relatively disease-free, although it is not possible for all of us to achieve such an ideal state all of the time. Perhaps we should all start taking note of the old saying, 'Look on the bright side.'

Certainly it is the case that a miserable frame of mind, of the kind that follows some kind of personal tragedy, can lead to physical disorder. Since there is some scientific evidence that in the latter case the brain has been at work and that chemical substances that have a suppressive effect on the immune system have been released, it is possible that a chemical substance is also released in response to a happy frame of mind that will have a stimulating, boosting effect on the immune system.

The role of a happy frame of mind in keeping us well

has been recognized as far back as biblical times. According to the Bible, 'a merry heart doeth good like medicine'. Laughter, in particular, is now held by some to be particularly therapeutic.

The mind and recovery

The above is all very well if you are already well and are intent on remaining that way. However, what if, despite all your best efforts to stay cheerful, sensibly fed, and well-exercised, you have fallen victim to some illness. Can your mind help you there?

The answer to this has been answered in part in the section above, "The mind and keeping well'. As has been mentioned, it would appear, that a happy, cheerful frame of mind seems to give one a better chance of keeping well than a miserable, sad one.

It follows from that, and would appear to be frequently the case, that people who have been ill or injured have a tendency to get better more quickly than someone who is in a neutral frame of mind and certainly more quickly than someone who is in a miserable, depressed state. In the case of people who are unhappy, especially following a sad life event, it has been mentioned in the first part of this chapter The mind and illness that scientific research suggests that some chemical released by the brain has damped down the immune system.

Placebo effect and healing

Some of the information given in the section on 'Placebo' under The Mind and Illness is relevant here. As has been pointed out in that section, there are some people who feel sure that a certain substance will help to alleviate their pain or symptoms and claim that such an alleviation has been brought about even although, unknown to them, the said substance is totally inactive and harmless.

Thus belief in a cure seems sometimes to be able to help to cure a disorder. As has been mentioned, as a result of the placebo effect the seeming alleviation of symptoms is possibly because of the release of certain chemicals from the brain, similar to those released when pain is suppressed for a time.

The placebo effect may be an element in seemingly successful faith healing. The person who has sought the help of a faith healer believes that his or her touch will effect some sort of cure, and indeed the patient does sometimes find it has helped, or claims to do so. There is a good deal of scepticism around in relation to faith healing, but only the patient can tell if it has been in any way effective.

This same placebo effect seems to be at work in some of the seemingly successful cures, or at least in the successful alleviation or remission of symptoms, that people claim to have experienced at one of the places of pilgrimage that are noted for their healing powers.

The most famous of these is Lourdes in France, where in February 1858 a fourteen-year-old peasant girl named Bernadette Soubirous saw what she said was an apparition in the form of the Virgin Mary. This apparition directed her to a spring in a muddy grotto, which became the supposed miracle cure that still draws thousands of people to Lourdes.

There have been many thousands of recorded cases of alleged miracle cures at Lourdes, but fewer than a hundred of these have been recognized as miraculous by the Roman Catholic Church. Some of these cures may well be attributable to the fact that modern medicine effected the cure, some to the fact that the patient's own immune system overcame the disease eventually and quite a few to the placebo effect.

In the case of faith or spiritual healing the patient does not appear to have to have any religious faith for some kind of alleviation of symptoms to occur. Spiritual healers themselves may regard their skill as having come from God or from the spirit world but the patient need not necessarily share this belief.

Cases have been recorded in which there was no particular belief or faith on either side, patient or healer, and yet it is claimed that some kind of curative process took place. This kind of case might occur when a person touches someone who is ill and discovers that he or she has been cured, or claims to have been cured. Such a person might then well go on to set up as a psychic healer.

Some psychic healers claim to be able to see an aura round people and say that any disturbance in this is an indication of illness of some kind. There are some psychic healers who claim to see silver lines and spots mapped out on people's bodies, which indicate the source of pain or illness, and who claim that touching a spot where a light shows effects a cure. This spot is quite frequently in a different part of the body from that in which the patient feels the pain.

Psychic healers are met with a great deal of scepticism. Anything out of the ordinary, certainly anything that suggests the paranormal, often meets with the same response.

Obviously no one knows the source of the psychic healer's gift, if such exists, but there are patients who claim to have been cured by this gift. Some degree of success may again be able to be put down to the placebo effect, to the fact that the patient has a belief, sometimes a belief born of sheer desperation, sometimes a belief born of the fact that he or she has heard of someone else who has been cured by the healer, that the psychic healer can help him or her.

It is quite common for psychic healers to be held to be charlatans. Possibly some of them are, but then there are charlatans to be found in most walks of life. As long as no active harm is done and no excessive fees are charged or excessive claims made, it seems to me that anything than can be done for the physical or mental being of patients for whom all else has failed has got to be looked at in a positive light.

Think positively

There is a growing belief even among members of the

medical profession that a patient's positive attitude towards disease may boost the body's defence system against it. This could perhaps be due to an effect on the immune system by the brain.

For example, some studies of women who survive breast cancer that has been diagnosed in its relatively early stages suggest that women who demonstrate a determination to get better and a fighting spirit to defeat the cancer survive longer and lead more normal lives than those who seem completely overwhelmed by the disease. This is yet another example of the mind exerting its influence in our lives.

However, this is not the whole story. There are many cases of women who had everything to live for—mothers of several young children, for example—who were full of fighting spirit and determination to defeat the dread disease but who did not survive very long after having had the cancer diagnosed and after treatment.

An attitude of mind may help. However, most doctors agree that physical factors relating to the cancer, such as the nature of the tumour, the location of the tumour, the age of the woman, matter more.

It would be quite wrong to suggest that a woman who does not survive breast cancer, or indeed anyone who does not survive a major disease or an injury of any kind, was lacking in the will to live or the fighting spirit. This would place a totally unfair and unjustified burden of guilt on someone who is dying.

Sometimes there is just nothing the mind can do. It can

be a powerful influence, but there are other influences at
work also and sometimes the body defeats it.

Curing the body through the mind

The mind is sometimes involved in the treatment of disease, not only of mental disease but of some forms of
physical disease. This is particularly true of hypnosis,
which is sometimes used in the treatment of pain.

Hypnosis seems to direct our attention away from pain
and so blocks off our perception of it. It can also be used
in curing persistent skin rashes as well as in trying to
cure addiction to smoking, insomnia and various other
disorders.

Hypnosis frequently receives a very bad press. It is often associated in people's minds with stage or television
shows in which people are made to appear foolish.
There may be some charlatans in hypnosis, as indeed
there are in most walks of life, but there are many extremely skilled hypnotists around who use their skills
for therapeutic purposes. Many members of the medical
profession recognize that hypnosis can play a part in the
recovery of patients, and some of them will recommend
a hypnotist to their patients.

Many people are afraid of being hypnotized and think
that when a person is in a hypnotic state he or she is actually asleep, but this is not the case. Hypnosis is not
sleep. It is more a state in which a person withdraws
from the normal state of consciousness but does not yet
reach the unconscious state.

It is like a borderline state between consciousness and unconsciousness that acts as a link between those two states. When people are in a hypnotic state to some extent they remain aware and deeply absorbed but are in a state in which one is open to hypnotic suggestion, although some people are easier to put under hypnosis than others.

Psychotherapy and psychoanalysis

Psychotherapy or psychoanalysis, both forms of treatment that work on the mind, are sometimes used to try to cure disorders of the body as well as disorders of the mind itself, showing how important the mind is to general health. These physical disorders may be thought to have some psychological background or cause.

In psychotherapy and psychoanalysis the patient is encouraged to talk spontaneously about all the things that have happened in his or her life since early childhood. It has been mentioned above in the section on hysteria that it was the treatment of 'Anna O' by Josef Breuer, colleague of Sigmund Freud, that led to the development of psychoanalysis. 'Anna O' was suffering from various forms of paralysis and part of Breuer's treatment was to get her to tell him all about her life so that he could identify anything that might have led to the hysteria.

Summary

Thus the mind can be a force for good as well as ill. It can be involved in curing as well as causing illness.

Something has been learnt about the possible mechanics of this but there is much still to learn and possibly much that will never be fully understood or rationalized. The mind and the exact source and range of its power is likely to remain something of an enigma in relation to health and illness as in other cases.

Bibliography

Ahead of Time Dennis Bardens, Robert Hale 1991

Explaining the Unexplained Hans J. Eysenck and Carl Sargent, Prion 1993

Marvels and Mysteries of the Human Mind The Reader's Digest Association Ltd 1992

Mind Waves Betty Shine, Transworld 1993

Mysteries of the Mind Reuben Stone, Blitz Editions 1993

Poltergeists and the Paranormal Reuben Stone, Blitz editions 1993

The Mind Machine Colin Blakemore, BBC Books 1988

The Paranormal—A Modern Perspective John Spencer, Hamlyn 1992

Index